# MAC OS X PANTHER

NICK VANDOME

BARNES
&NOBLE
BOOKS
NEW YORK

**In easy steps** is an imprint of Computer Step
Southfield Road . Southam
Warwickshire CV47 0FB . United Kingdom
www.ineasysteps.com

This edition published for Barnes & Noble Books, New York
FOR SALE IN THE USA ONLY
www.bn.com

**Notice of Liability**
Every effort has been made to ensure that this book contains
accurate and current information. However, Computer Step and the
author shall not be liable for any loss or damage suffered by readers
as a result of any information contained herein.

**Trademarks**
Mac OS X® is a registered trademark of Apple Computer, Inc. All
other trademarks are acknowledged as belonging to their respective
companies.

Printed and bound in the United Kingdom

ISBN  0-7607-5736-4

# Contents

## Maintaining OS X                  175

## 10

## Index                            187

# Introducing OS X Panther

OS X Panther is the latest operating system from Apple Computers. It is promoted as being easy and enjoyable to use and also incredibly stable for a computer operating system. This chapter introduces OS X, shows you how to obtain and install it and also some of its fundamental features.

## Covers

Chapter One

# About OS X

In 1984 Apple Computers introduced a new operating system (OS) for its Macintosh computers and, at the time, it was revolutionary. Instead of having to access programs and files through lines of lengthy computer code commands, users could navigate their way through Apple computers using a new Graphical User Interface (GUI). This produced the same results as the previous method, but it was much easier for the user: instead of having to type in lines of computer coding it was possible to access files and programs by clicking on buttons, icons and drop down menus. This ease of use was a major factor in the mass adoption of personal computers and this type of operating system soon began to appear on all personal computers, not just Macs.

*Apple Computers have always been known for their ease of use and OS X takes this to a new level. In addition, it also makes it a lot easier for users to share files between Macs and Windows based PCs. This has been a problem in the past and with OS X the barriers between the two sets of computer users have been broken down to a certain degree.*

Over the years Apple refined its OS and added more and more functions with each new release. However, like any operating system the Mac OS was not without its problems: it was as prone to crashes as any other operating system and it had its own quirky idiosyncrasies, such as extension conflicts (when two programs refused to cohabit on the same machine).

When Apple decided to upgrade their OS from version 9 they were faced with two choices: add more code to what was becoming an incredibly complicated structure for the Apple programmers to work with, or, create an entirely new program from scratch. Thankfully, they chose the second option, and the result is OS X.

*UNIX is an operating system that has traditionally been used for large commercial mainframe computers. It is renowned for its stability and ability to be used within different computing environments.*

In some ways OS X is a contradiction of Apple's original philosophy: while it retains and enhances its traditional ease of use, it is also based on the UNIX programming language, the very type of thing that Apple was trying to get away from in 1984. The reason it is based on UNIX is that this is a very stable operating environment and this ensures that OS X is one of the most stable consumer operating systems that has ever been designed. (This is one claim that appears to be true and is not just marketing hype.) However, for most users, they can be blissfully unaware of the very existence of UNIX if they want and just enjoy its benefits while using the new Aqua interface of OS X and all of the advantages that this brings. For the programming expert, there is also an option of delving into UNIX itself and getting to grips with this side of the program.

# Obtaining OS X

*Mac OS X is pre-installed on all new Mac computers including the iMac, iBook and eMac.*

OS X is widely available from Apple stores, stockists and some software retailers. It can also be ordered directly from the Apple website at www.apple.com. To order OS X from the Apple site:

1 Click on the Mac OS X tab on the Apple website and click on the Buy Now button

*OS X cannot be downloaded from the Apple site. It has to be ordered and it will then be delivered. However, if there are updates to an existing version, these will be available for download from the website.*

2 Click here to add OS X to your order

3 Proceed to the checkout and complete the payment details for OS X

# Installing OS X

The first step to install OS X is to insert the CD-ROM into the CD drive. The disk should run automatically and the installation can then proceed as follows:

1 Double-click here to read any last-minute release notes

*Make sure you read any of the online documentation before you install OS X. These documents, which are usually in PDF format, can contain useful general information and also any late news about the program that was released after it was produced.*

|  | Welcome to Mac OS X | |
|---|---|---|
| | 18 items, 13.8 MB available | |

**Read Before You Install.pdf**

**Install Mac OS X**

**Optional Installs**

**Utilities**

**Dansk**

**Deutsch**

**Español**

2 Double-click on the Install Mac OS X icon to begin the installation process

**3** Enter a name and password

**4** Click OK

*The name and password that is entered at the beginning of the installation process will be needed if you want to set up your computer for multiple users. For more details on this, see Chapter Eight. In some cases, a password is also required for installing software updates.*

**5** Click Restart. Your computer will then shut down and start up again and take you through the rest of the registration process

*The registration process consists of entering a few details and then moving through a series of dialog windows. In most cases all you have to do is accept the default settings and options that are displayed.*

# The OS X environment

The first most noticeable element about OS X is its elegant user interface. This has been designed to create a user friendly graphic overlay to the UNIX operating system at the heart of OS X and it is a combination of rich colors and sharp, original graphics. The main elements that make up the initial OS X environment are:

Apple menu    Menu bar    Windows    Disk icons

The Dock    Desktop

# Aqua interface

The name given by Apple to its OS X interface is Aqua. This describes the graphical appearance of the operating system. Essentially, it is just the cosmetic appearance of the elements within the operating system, but they combine to give OS X a rich visual look and feel. Some of the main elements of the Aqua interface are:

### Menus

*The graphics used in OS X are designed in a style known as Quartz.*

Menus in OS X contain commands for the operating system and any relevant programs. If there is an arrow next to a command it means there are subsequent options for the item:

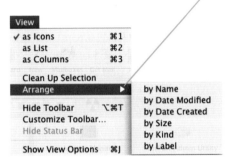

### Window buttons

These appear in any open OS X window and can be used to manipulate the window.

*If OS X has no preferred option in a dialog box, all of the option buttons are grey. However, it is still possible to click on the button of your choice.*

### Option buttons

Whenever a dialog box with separate options is accessed, OS X highlights the suggested option with a pulsing blue button. This can be accepted by clicking on it or by pressing Enter. If you do not want to accept this option, click on another button in the dialog box.

# Running OS 9 and OS X

Even though OS X is up to version 3 (10.3), there are still a lot of users operating programs that were written before the appearance of OS X. Apple overcomes this by bundling the previous operating system, OS 9, with OS X. OS 9 is automatically installed along with OS X. This means that there are in effect two operating systems on the same computer. For newer programs OS X will automatically be used to open and run them, but for older ones, OS 9 will open up and run the programs. This is known as opening programs in Classic mode. This happens automatically when you open a program that is not able to run on OS X: the OS 9 environment will open and run the program.

*Programs that were written for OS 9 and have not been updated at all are known as Classic programs. Programs written for OS 9 but amended so that they can be opened by OS X are known as Carbon programs. Programs written specifically for OS X are known as Cocoa programs.*

If you previously ran OS 9 on your computer it is possible to see the contents of your old desktop by double-clicking on the Desktop Mac OS 9, located on the OS X desktop. The contents of the OS 9 desktop are then available, exactly as they were before OS X was installed:

*There is an increasing number of Cocoa programs becoming available for use with OS X and it is an area in which software companies are investing heavily.*

# Classic mode

If programs are not compatible with OS X they will open in Classic mode, i.e. with OS 9. This happens automatically and it is not always possible to know in which mode a program will open until you access it. In general, programs that were previously used in OS 9, and have not been upgraded, will open in Classic mode. To open a program in Classic mode:

*Even if programs open in Classic mode, their icons can still be placed on the OS X Dock. For more details on the Dock, see Chapter Two.*

1 Open a program from the OS 9 desktop folder or from the Dock

Dreamweaver 4 alias

2 Classic mode is activated to open the program. This takes a few seconds

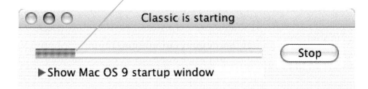

3 The program opens in Classic mode, i.e. with OS 9, and it can then be used in the same way as any other program, except that it does not have the OS X user interface

*Any programs that you had under a previous Mac operating system should run in Classic mode on a computer using OS X.*

# Booting up in OS 9 and OS X

### Booting up in OS 9

In some circumstances you may want to boot up your computer in OS 9 which means it opens in exactly the same way as before OS X was installed. You may want to do this if a particular program does not open up in Classic mode or if you do not have the OS X drivers for devices such as Zip drives and printers (these may not work in OS X, but they probably will if you boot up in OS 9). To do this:

1 Select System Preferences>Startup Disk and click here

*If you have problems in OS X with items such as external drives or printers, it could be because you do not have the correct OS X drivers installed. One option in this instance is to boot up in OS 9 and use the device with the older versions of the drivers. However, it makes sense to download the updated drivers as soon as possible. To do this, visit the Web site of the company that manufactured the affected device.*

2 Click Restart. When the computer reboots, it will be in OS 9

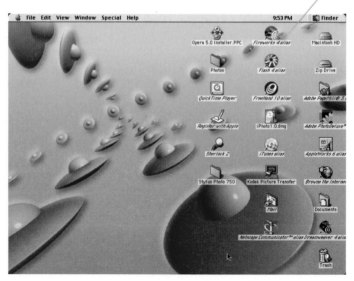

## Returning to OS X

To return to OS X from OS 9:

1 Select Apple menu>Control Panels>Startup Disk from the menu bar

*Always set OS X as the default for booting up your computer, unless you have a good reason not to.*

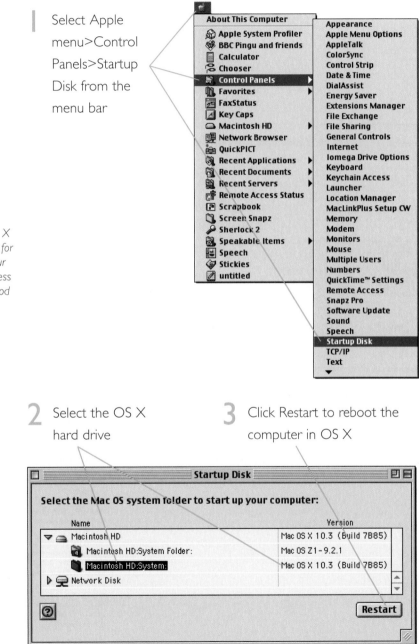

2 Select the OS X hard drive

3 Click Restart to reboot the computer in OS X

# Background on UNIX

UNIX is the powerful and robust operating system that is the foundation on which OS X runs. In fact, OS X is essentially a very impressive graphical interface placed on top of a version of UNIX known as Darwin.

UNIX was developed in the early 1970s by programmers who wanted to design an operating system that could run on any platform, i.e. different types of computers. Up until then, each operating system had generally been designed for a specific type of computer. Another benefit of UNIX was that it was designed to be available to the whole development community. The program that was used to create UNIX is the now widely used C language.

UNIX first gained popularity in academic institutions and it was then taken on by government organizations. Its adoption by Apple as the foundation for OS X has seen UNIX move into the mainstream of consumer computing. UNIX's greatest strength is its stability, while its greatest weakness is perhaps its non-user-friendliness. Apple have made the most of the former and overcome the latter with its Aqua interface and Quartz graphics.

*In addition to OS X on consumer computers Apple have also released a new server that runs on UNIX. This is called XServer and it is used to run and manage computer networks.*

For people with experience of UNIX, programming can be performed within OS X in the Terminal window. This is the gateway into the UNIX environment and it can be located in Applications>Utilities from the Finder. If you are not familiar with UNIX, you need never worry about it or the Terminal again.

Working with UNIX in the Terminal is not for the uninitiated, or the faint-hearted

```
Welcome to Darwin!
Nick-Vandomes-eMac:~ nickvandome$ cd Documents
Nick-Vandomes-eMac:~/Documents nickvandome$ ls
Acting.dvdproj          Singing.dvdproj         test
2 2.dvdproj
AppleWorks User Data    Summer.dvdproj          test
2.dvdproj
My Great DVD.dvdproj    holidays_dvd.dvdproj
Saddell_2004.dvdproj    test2 1.dvdproj
Nick-Vandomes-eMac:~/Documents nickvandome$ cd movie
s
-bash: cd: movies: No such file or directory
Nick-Vandomes-eMac:~/Documents nickvandome$ cd "Appl
eworks User Data"
Nick-Vandomes-eMac:~/Documents/Appleworks User Data
nickvandome$ ls
AutoSave        Starting Points
Nick-Vandomes-eMac:~/Documents/Appleworks User DaNic
Nick-Vandomes-eMac:~/Documents/Appleworks User Data
nickvandome$
```

Terminal — bash — 52x20

# Shutting down

The Apple menu (which can be accessed by clicking on the Apple icon at the top left corner of the desktop or any subsequent OS X window) has been standardized in OS X. This means that it has the same options regardless of the program in which you are working. This has a number of advantages, not least is the fact that it makes it easier to shut down your Mac. When shutting down, there are three options that can be selected:

- Sleep. This puts the Mac into hibernation mode, i.e. the screen goes blank and the hard drive becomes inactive. This state is maintained until the mouse is moved or a key is pressed on the keyboard. This then wakes up the Mac and it is ready to continue work

- Restart. This closes down the Mac and then restarts it again. This can be useful if you have added new software and your computer requires a restart to make it active

- Shut Down. This closes down the Mac completely once you have finished working

*When shutting down, make sure you have saved all of your open documents, although OS X will prompt you to do this if you have forgotten.*

*If you install new software you will usually have to restart your computer before it takes effect.*

Click here to access the Apple menu

Click here to access one of the shut down options

# OS X Help

Although the online help is not the most extensive that has ever been produced, it does provide some useful assistance for using OS X. To access the Help files:

1 Select Help> Mac Help from the Menu bar

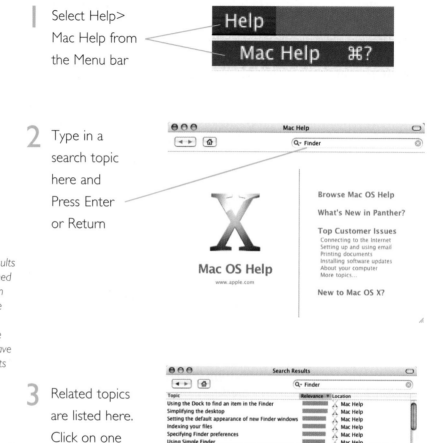

2 Type in a search topic here and Press Enter or Return

*The search results that are returned from a query in OS X Help are not always an exact match for what you are looking for. Sometimes you have to scroll down the list of results to find a particular item.*

3 Related topics are listed here. Click on one to see a summary of it or double-click on it to see its full entry

# Up and running with OS X

This chapter looks at some of the features of OS X that can help you get up and running quickly with the operating system. These include the Dock for organizing and accessing all of the elements of the computer, the system preferences for the way the computer looks and operates and also working with items on the desktop.

## Covers

**Chapter Two**

# Introducing the Dock

The Dock is one of the main innovative elements of OS X. Its main function is to help organize and access programs, folders and files. In addition, with its rich translucent colors and elegant graphical icons, it also makes an aesthetically pleasing addition to the desktop. The main things to remember about the Dock are:

*The Dock is always displayed as a line of icons, but this can be orientated either vertically or horizontally.*

- It is divided into two: programs go on the left of the dividing line; all other items go on the right

- It can be edited in just about any way you choose

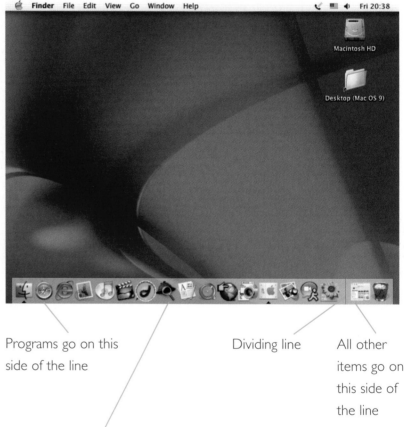

*Items on the Dock can be opened by clicking on them once, rather than having to double-click on them.*

Programs go on this side of the line

Dividing line

All other items go on this side of the line

By default the Dock appears at the bottom of the screen

# Setting Dock preferences

As with most elements of OS X, the Dock can be modified in numerous ways. This can affect both the appearance of the Dock and the way it operates. To set Dock preferences:

*The Apple menu is constantly available in OS X, regardless of the program in which you are working. The menu options are also constant in all applications.*

1 Select Apple menu>Dock from the menu bar

*You will not be able to make the Dock size too large so that some of the icons would not be visible on the desktop. By default, the Dock is resized so that everything is always visible.*

2 Select the general preferences here

3 Click here to access more Dock preferences

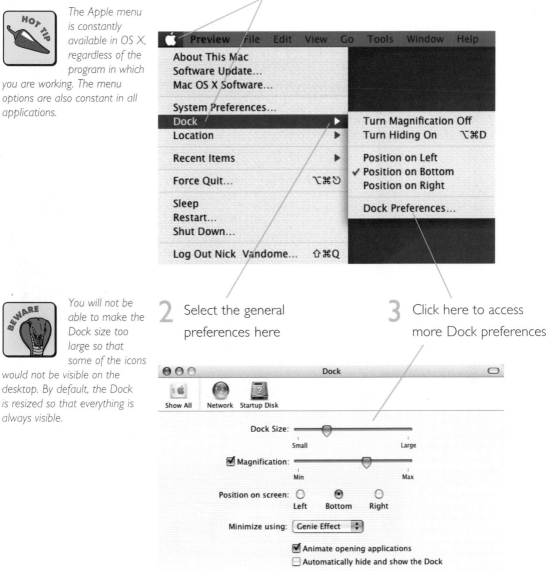

The Dock Preferences allow you to change its size, orientation, the way icons appear and effects for when items are minimized:

The "Position on screen" options enable you to place the Dock on the left, right or bottom of the screen

Drag the Dock Size slider to increase or decrease the size of the Dock

*The Dock always sits on top of any open windows. You may therefore want to move its position if it obscures part of an open window. This can sometimes be an issue if the Dock is positioned at the bottom of the screen.*

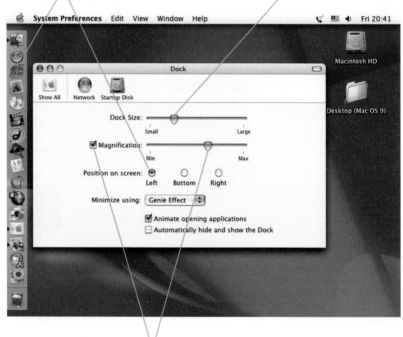

*The Dock cannot be moved by dragging it, this can only be done in the Dock Preferences window.*

Check on the Magnification box and drag the slider to determine the size to which icons are enlarged when the cursor is moved over them

When the cursor is moved over an item in the Dock, the name of that item is displayed above it.

**...cont'd**

The effects that are applied to items when they are minimized is one of the features of OS X (it is not absolutely necessary but it sums up the Apple ethos of trying to enhance the user experience as much as possible).

The Genie effect shrinks the item to be minimized like a genie going back into its lamp

*The other animated effect for minimizing open windows is the Scale effect, where the window scales itself down proportionately to fit on the Dock.*

*Open windows can also be minimized by double-clicking on their title bar (the thinly lined bar at the top of the window, next to the three window buttons.)*

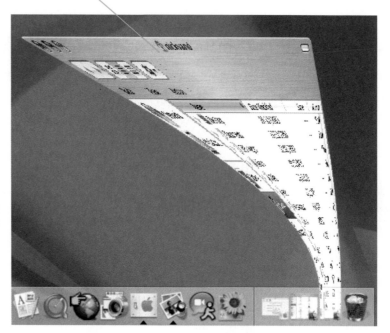

### Manual resizing
In addition to changing the size of the Dock by using the Dock Preference dialog box, it can also be resized manually:

Drag vertically on the Dock dividing line to increase or decrease its size

# Accessing items

The Dock can be used to access everything within your Mac computer. In most cases it will be the starting point before you start any new operation or project. It can be used to open programs, access programs that are already open or access open documents or folders.

*While an item is opening, its icon bobs up and down on the Dock.*

*Once an item has been opened from the Dock, its applications, folders or files can be opened by double-clicking on them.*

*Due to the power of OS X, numerous programs can be open and running at the same time, without affecting the overall memory of your computer. This is because OS X assigns all of the available memory to the active program, i.e. the one that is being worked with. If you switch to another program, the memory is assigned to that one, and so on.*

2 The selected item opens in a new window. Each new item selected from the Dock opens in its own window

1 Click once on an item on the Dock to open it

3 Once an item has been opened, a black triangle appears below it. This only disappears once the item is closed

# Dock menus

One of the features of the Dock is that it can display contextual menus for selected items. This means that it shows menus with options that are applicable to the item that is being accessed. This can only be done when an item has been opened.

*If the selected item is a program, any open files will be displayed in the item's Dock contextual menu. Click on a file to access it directly.*

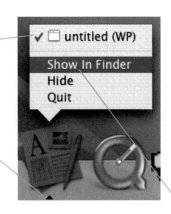

Click and hold here to display an item's individual menu

*Click on Quit on the Dock's contextual menu to close an open program or file, depending on which side of the dividing bar the item is located.*

2 Click on Show In Finder to see where the item is located on your computer

*For a more detailed look at the workings of the Finder, see Chapter Three.*

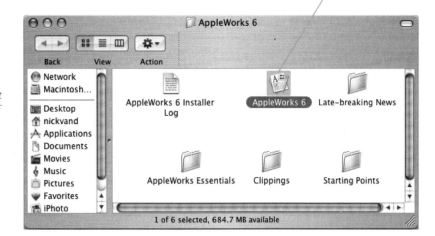

# Trash

The Trash folder is a location for placing items that you do not want to use anymore. However, when items are placed in the Trash, they are not removed from your computer. This requires another command, as the Trash is really a holding area before you decide you want to remove items permanently. The Trash can also be used for ejecting removable disks attached to your Mac.

### Sending items to the Trash

Items can be sent to the Trash by dragging them from the location in which they are stored:

*Items can also be sent to the Trash by selecting them and then selecting File>Move to Trash from the Menu bar.*

1 Drag an item over the Trash icon to place it in the Trash folder

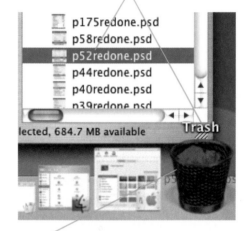

*All of the items within the Trash can be removed in a single command: Select Finder>Empty Trash from the Menu bar to remove all of the items in the Trash folder.*

2 Click once on the Trash icon on the Dock to view its contents

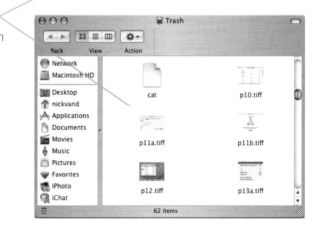

*If you select the Empty Trash option this removes all of the items in the Trash folder permanently. If you choose to do this, check all of the items in the Trash to make sure you are not removing something that you still need.*

# Adding and removing Dock items

## Adding items

As many items as you like can be added to the Dock; the only restriction is the size of monitor in which to display all of the Dock items (the size of the Dock can be reduced to accommodate more icons but you have to be careful that all of the icons are still legible). To add items to the Dock:

*Icons on the Dock are shortcuts to the related item, rather than the item itself, which remains in its original location.*

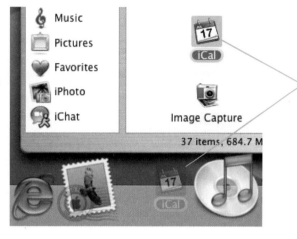

Locate the required item and drag it onto the Dock. All of the other icons move along to make space for the new one

*You can add as many items as you like to the Dock, but it will automatically shrink to display all of its items if it becomes too big for the available monitor space.*

## Keep in Dock

Everytime you open a new program, its icon will appear in the Dock for the duration that the program is open, even if it has not previously been put in the Dock. If you then decide that you would like to keep it in the Dock, you can do so as follows:

2 Click on Keep In Dock to ensure the program remains in the Dock when it is closed

Click and hold on the black triangle underneath an open program

### Removing items

Any item, except the Finder, can be removed from the Dock. However, this does not remove it from our computer, it just removes the shortcut for accessing it. You will still be able to locate it in its folder on your hard drive and, if required, drag it back onto the Dock. To remove items from the Dock:

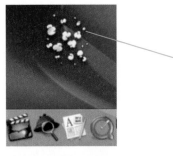

Drag it away from the Dock and release. The item disappears in a satisfying puff of smoke to indicate that it has been removed. All of the other icons then move up to fill in the space

*Removing an item from the Dock, does not affect the actual item in any way. All it does is remove the shortcut to that item. It is still in its original location and its original format.*

### Removing open programs

You can remove a program from the Dock, even if it is open and running. To do this:

1 Drag a program off the Dock while it is running. Initially the icon will remain on the Dock because the program is still open

2 When the program is closed its icon will be removed from the Dock

# System Preferences

In OS X there are preferences that can be set for just about every aspect of the program. This gives you great control over how the interface looks and how the operating system functions. To access System Preferences:

Click on this icon on the Dock or from the Applications folder in the Finder

## Personal preferences

Appearance. Options for the overall look of buttons, menus, windows and scroll bars.

Desktop & Screen Saver. This can be used to change the desktop background and the screen saver.

Dock. Options for the way the Dock looks and functions.

Exposé. This can be used to specify keystrokes for the different Exposé functions. (For more details, see page 35.)

International. Options for the language used on the computer.

Security. This enables you to secure your Home folder with a master password, for added security.

## Hardware preferences

CDs & DVDs. Options for what action is taken when you insert CDs and DVDs.

Displays. Options for the screen display, such as resolution.

Energy Saver. Options for when the computer is inactive.

Keyboard & Mouse. Options for how the keyboard and mouse function and also keyboard shortcuts.

Print & Fax. Options for selecting printers and handling faxes.

Sound. Options for adding sound effects and playing and recording sound.

*The Security preferences use a function called FileVault to protect the contents of your hard drive by encrypting the information, which can be protected by your login password and also by a master password for your computer. However, if you forget your login password and the master password is not available, you will not be able to access your data. In general, FileVault should not be used unless you have genuine concerns about the security of your computer.*

### Internet & Network preferences

.Mac. Options for setting up your online .Mac membership and also for configuring your iDisk. This is looked at in more detail in Chapter Seven.

Network. This can be used to specify network setting for linking two or more computers together. This is looked at in more detail in Chapter Nine.

*Items within System Preferences can be added to the System Preferences toolbar by dragging them from the main window, in the same way as adding them to the Dock or the Finder toolbar.*

QuickTime. Options for configuring the QuickTime Player for playing movies and music.

Sharing. This can be used to specify how files are shared over a network. This is also looked at in Chapter Nine.

### System preferences

Accounts. This can be used to allow different users to create their own accounts for use on the same computer.

Classic. Options for how the Classic environment operates when a pre-OS X program is launched.

Date & Time. Options for changing the computer's date and time.

Software Update. This can be used to specify how software updates are handled. It can be set so that updates are automatically downloaded when the computer is connected to the Internet.

Speech. Options for using speakable commands to control the computer. This can be useful for users who find it uncomfortable using the keyboard or the mouse as it enables them to perform some tasks by speech alone.

Startup Disk. This can be used to specify the disk from which your computer starts up. This is usually the OS X volume, or in some cases, a previous version of the Mac operating system.

Universal Access. This can be used to set options for users who have difficulty with viewing text on screen, hearing commands, using the keyboard or using the mouse. There are options for each of these areas which make it possible for as wide a range of users as possible to get the most out of OS X.

# Desktop items

If required, the Desktop can be used to store programs and files. However, the Finder (see Chapter Three) does such a good job of organizing all of the elements within your computer that the Desktop is rendered largely redundant, unless you feel happier storing items here. The Desktop also displays any removable disks that are connected to your computer.

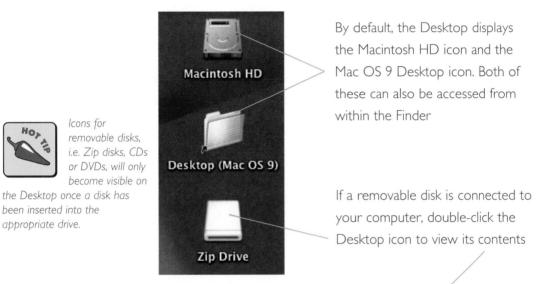

By default, the Desktop displays the Macintosh HD icon and the Mac OS 9 Desktop icon. Both of these can also be accessed from within the Finder

 *Icons for removable disks, i.e. Zip disks, CDs or DVDs, will only become visible on the Desktop once a disk has been inserted into the appropriate drive.*

If a removable disk is connected to your computer, double-click the Desktop icon to view its contents

*Any removable disks that are connected to your computer can also be viewed by clicking on them in the Sidebar in the Finder.*

# Ejecting items

In previous versions of the Mac operating system, external disks could only be ejected by the slightly unusual method of dragging their icon over the Trash. However, although this still remains available it is also now possible to eject external disks directly from the Finder.

### Ejecting with the Finder

*Volumes are any individual areas for storing data, such as the hard drive on your computer, connected networks, your iDisk or external drives such as a Zip drive or a CD.*

Click here to eject an external disk

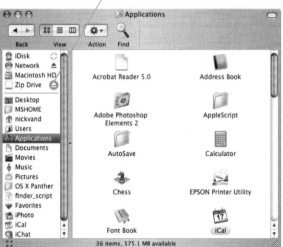

*Ejecting with the Trash can still be a useful option if the Finder window is not immediately available i.e. it is minimized or hidden behind other windows.*

### Ejecting with the Trash

If you like the way things used to be done, you can still eject external disks by dragging them over the Trash:

Drag the disk's icon from the Desktop and drop it onto the Trash icon on the Dock. Release the mouse button when the word Eject appears

# Organizing with Exposé

Exposé is a unique function within OS X Panther that enables you to quickly organize and display all of your open files and programs. It can be applied to all of the items on your desktop or to a single specific program and its files. By default, Exposé is operated by the F (function) keys. To do this:

## Organizing your desktop

When working with a lot of files and programs, the desktop can become cluttered very quickly

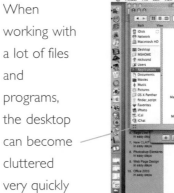

*Click once on any window to activate it and return it to its original size.*

2 Press F9 to display all of the individual items that are open on the desktop. Press F9 again to return to the previous state

*Pass the cursor over an item that has been revealed by Exposé to see its name.*

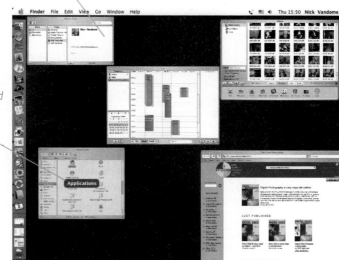

## Organizing within a program

If there are a lot of open files within a single program, Exposé can be used to view all of the files on the desktop. The files are sized to accommodate them all within the available workspace. To so this:

| In a single program, open files are stacked on top of one another

2 Press F10 to display all of the individual items that are open on the desktop. Press F10 again to return to the previous state

*Press F11 to hide all of the open documents and programs on the desktop. This reveals a completely clear desktop. Press F11 again to restore all of the hidden items.*

# Finder

The principal program for moving around OS X is the Finder. This enables you to access items and organize your programs, folders and files. This chapter looks at how to use the Finder and how to get the most out of this powerful tool that is at the heart of navigating around OS X.

## Covers

Chapter Three

# Working with the Finder

If you were only able to use one item on the Dock it would be the Finder. This is the gateway to all of the elements of your computer. It is possible to get to selected items through other routes, but the Finder is the only location where you can gain access to everything on your system. If you ever feel that you are getting lost within OS X, click on the Finder and then you should begin to feel more at home. To access the Finder:

Click once on this
icon on the Dock

## Overview

*The Finder is always open (as denoted by the black triangle underneath its icon on the Dock) and it cannot readily be closed down or removed.*

The Finder has its own toolbar, a Sidebar from which items can be accessed and a main window where the contents of selected items can be viewed:

*The Action button has options for displaying information about a selected item and also options for how it is displayed with the Finder.*

Forward and Back buttons

View options

Action button

Toolbar

Static and removable volumes are displayed here

Folders are displayed here

Sidebar

Main window

# Finder folders

## Home

This contains the contents of your own home directory, containing your personal folders and files. OS X inserts some pre-named folders which it thinks will be useful, but it is possible to rename, rearrange or delete these as you please. It is also possible to add as many more folders as you want.

*Your Home folder is a good one to add to the Dock, so that all of your own programs, folders and files are accessible with a single click.*

Click here to access the contents of your Home folder

48 items, 43.55 GB available

*When you are creating documents OS X, by default, recognizes their type and then, when you save them, suggests the most applicable folder in your Home directory in which to save them. So, if you have created a word processed document, OS X will suggest you save it in Documents, if it is a photograph it will suggest Pictures, if it is a video it will suggest Movies, and so on. In all cases it is possible to change the default location suggested by OS X.*

The Home folder contains the Public folder that can be used to share files with other users if the computer is part of a network

## Applications

This folder contains some of the programs on your computer. However, by default, it is only the programs that come installed with OS X and not every program on your system. If you had programs that you used under a previous Mac operating system, these will be contained within the Desktop Mac OS 9 folder. (To access this, double-click on the Desktop Mac OS 9 folder icon on your own Desktop.) However, it is possible to add any of these programs to your Applications folder by opening the Desktop Mac OS 9 folder and then dragging items into the Applications folder.

*The Applications folder is another one that is worth adding to the Dock.*

*The Applications folder contains programs that are associated specifically with OS X. Other programs that you used with a previous Mac operating system will be located in the Desktop (Mac OS 9) folder on the desktop. However, new programs that are added will be loaded in the Applications folder too.*

Click here to access the contents of your Applications folder

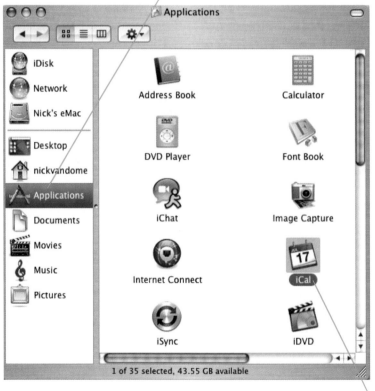

Double-click on an application icon to open the relevant program. This will open in its own, new, window

# Finder views

The way in which items are displayed within the Finder can be amended in a variety of ways, depending on how you want to view the contents of a folder. Different folders can have their own viewing options applied to them and these will stay in place until a new option is specified.

## Back button

When working within the Finder each new window replaces the previous one, unless you open a new program. This prevents the screen becoming cluttered with dozens of open windows, as you look through various Finder windows for a particular item. To ensure that you never feel lost within the Finder structure, there is a Back button on the Finder toolbar that enables you to retrace the steps that you have taken.

*If you have not opened any Finder windows, the Back button will not operate.*

1 Navigate to a folder within the Finder (in this case the Pictures folder contained within Documents)

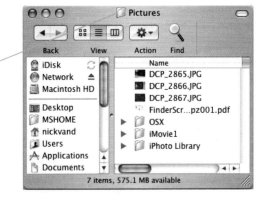

2 Click on the Back button to move back to the previously visited window (in this case, the main Documents window)

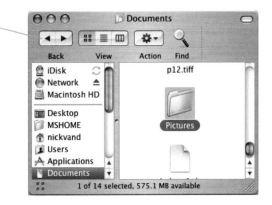

## Icon view

One of the viewing options for displaying items within the Finder is as icons. This provides a graphical description of the items in the Finder. It is possible to customize the way that icon view looks and functions:

*Icon view is a quick way to identify what items are, i.e. programs, folders, files, etc.*

**1** Click here on the Finder toolbar to access Icon View

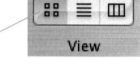

View

**2** Select View from the Menu bar, check on "as Icons" and select "Show View Options" to access the options for customizing icon view

| View | Go | Window | Help |
|---|---|---|---|
| ✓ as Icons | | | ⌘1 |
| as List | | | ⌘2 |
| as Columns | | | ⌘3 |
| Clean Up | | | |
| Arrange | | | ▶ |
| Hide Toolbar | | | ⌥⌘T |
| Customize Toolbar... | | | |
| Hide Status Bar | | | |
| Show View Options | | | ⌘J |

*Even with small icon sizes, icon view can make windows look rather cluttered, particularly if they contain a lot of items.*

*The Icon Arrangement options can be used to arrange icons into specific groups, e.g. by name or type, or to snap them to an invisible grid so that they have an ordered appearance.*

**Applications**

- ⦿ This window only
- ◯ All windows

Icon size: 32 x 32

Small ——— Large

Text size: 12 pt

Label position: ⦿ Bottom  ◯ Right

- ☐ Snap to grid
- ☐ Show item info
- ☐ Show icon preview
- ☑ Keep arranged by
  - Name

Background:
- ⦿ White
- ◯ Color
- ◯ Picture

Check on one of these options to specify the icon view for a specific window or all windows within Finder

Drag this slider to set the icon size

Select an option for the way icons are arranged in Finder windows (see Tip)

Select an option for the background of the Finder window

The icon size option (see previous page) can be used to increase or decrease the size of the icons within Finder windows:

*A very large icon size can be useful for people with poor eyesight, but it does take up a lot of space.*

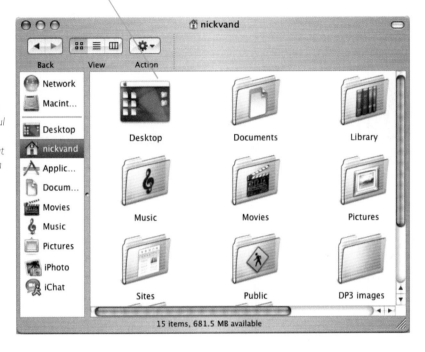

Select View>Clean Up from the Menu bar to put icons back in order if they have become disorganized over a period of time and use

## List view

List view can be used to show the items within a Finder window as a list, with additional information shown next to them. This can be a more efficient method than icon view if there are a lot of items within a folder: list view enables you to see more items at one time and also view the additional information:

*List view is a useful option once you feel comfortable with the way that the Finder functions.*

Click here on the Finder toolbar to access List view

*List view can be customized to include a variety of information such as file size and date last modified. Increase the window size (click on the green window button) to see all of the currently selected options.*

| Name | Date Modified | Size |
|------|---------------|------|
| ▶ Desktop | 10/12/2004 | -- |
| ▶ Documents | 04/11/2003 | -- |
| ▶ DP3 images | 12/02/2004 | -- |
| ▶ Library | 10/12/2003 | -- |
| ▶ Movies | 11/11/2003 | -- |
| ▶ Music | 04/11/2003 | -- |
| ▶ nickvandome.com | 11/04/2004 | -- |
| ▶ OS X text | 03/05/2004 | -- |
| ▶ OSX | 11/04/2004 | -- |
| ▶ Pictures | 10/12/2003 | -- |
| ▶ Public | 12/05/2004 | -- |
| Send Registration | 06/02/2004 | 4 KB |
| ▶ Server pages | 10/12/2004 | -- |
| ▶ Sites | 12/08/2004 | -- |
| Snapz Pro X License | 12/02/2004 | 4 KB |

nickvand

Back    View    Action

Network
Macint...
Desktop
nickvand
Applica...
Docum...
Movies
Music
Pictures
iPhoto
iChat

15 items, 681.5 MB available

*To see all of the List view options, select View>Show View Options from the Menu bar.*

The name of each folder or file is displayed here. If any item has additional elements within it, this is represented by a small triangle next to them (see next page)

Additional information in List view can include when the item was last modified and its size

If an item in List view has a small triangle next to it, click on the triangle to display the additional contents of the folder

*If you cannot find any item in the Finder, try using OS X's inbuilt search facility, located within the Finder. For more details, see page 49.*

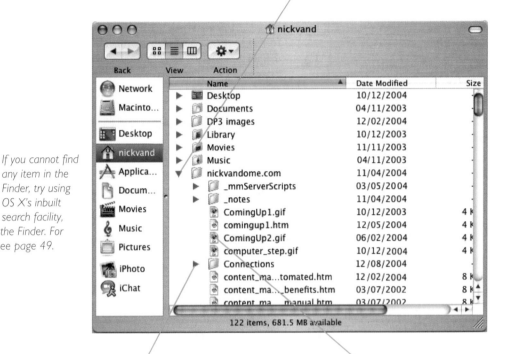

Keep clicking on triangles to drill down through the folder structure. If a triangle is pointing down, this indicates that its contents are displayed below it (and indented one step)

If items do not have any triangles next to them, this means that you have reached the bottom level of this particular folder structure (or a particular branch of a multi-level structure)

## Column view

Column view is a useful option if you want to trace the location of a particular item, i.e. see the full path of its location, starting from the Macintosh HD. This can help to give a better understanding of how OS X organizes the items within it.

Click here on the Finder toolbar to access Column view

*Column view is a good option for seeing the full path of the location of an item, i.e. where it is in relation to other items within the OS X structure.*

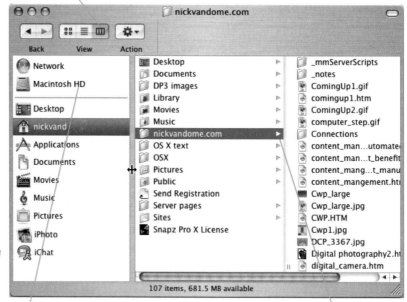

*The Column view window moves through each level as you trace the path of an item. For instance, if an item is five levels into a folder hierarchy, Column view will move through five panels until it displays the required item.*

Every selected item has a path that can be traced all the way back to the Macintosh HD

Click on an item to see everything within that folder. If an arrow follows an item it means that there are further items that can be viewed

# Finder toolbar

## Customizing the toolbar

As with most elements of OS X, it is possible to customize the Finder toolbar:

1 Select View> Customize Toolbar from the Menu bar

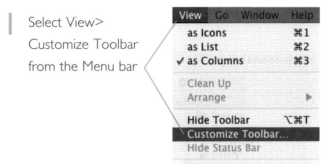

| View | Go | Window | Help |
| --- | --- | --- | --- |
| as Icons | | | ⌘1 |
| as List | | | ⌘2 |
| ✓ as Columns | | | ⌘3 |
| Clean Up | | | |
| Arrange | | | ▶ |
| Hide Toolbar | | | ⌥⌘T |
| Customize Toolbar... | | | |
| Hide Status Bar | | | |
| Show View Options | | | ⌘J |

*Do not put too many items on the Finder toolbar, because you may not be able to see them all in the Finder window. If there are additional toolbar items, there will be a directional arrow indicating this. Click on the arrow to view the items.*

2 Drag items from the window onto the toolbar, or:

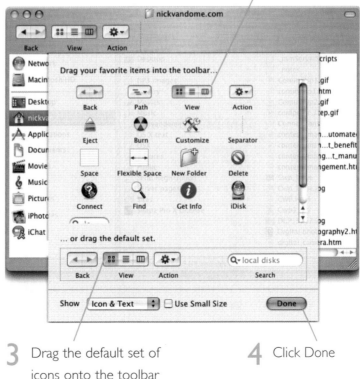

3 Drag the default set of icons onto the toolbar

4 Click Done

# Adding items to the Sidebar

Folders, programs and files can be added to the Finder Sidebar, in a similar way to adding them to the Dock. Once this has been done they are still available from their original location. To do this:

Drag an item from an open window and release it in the Finder Sidebar

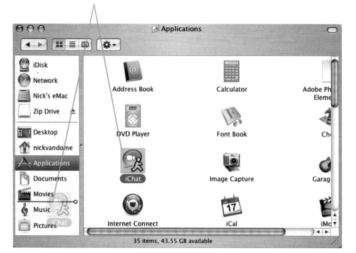

*When items are added to the Finder Sidebar a shortcut, or alias, is inserted into the Sidebar, not the actual item itself.*

2 The item can be accessed from the Sidebar and it is still located in its original location

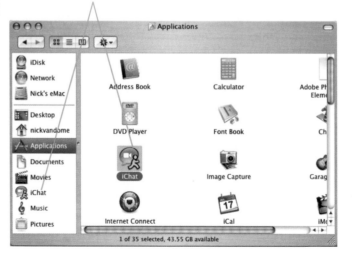

# Finder search

In previous Mac operating systems, items within the computer could be searched for using the Sherlock program. However, Sherlock is now used for searching the Internet (see Page 125) and the Mac search function has been incorporated in the Finder. The search box is one of the items that can be added to the toolbar as shown on page 47. To use the Finder search:

| Enter a search word or phrase here and press Enter

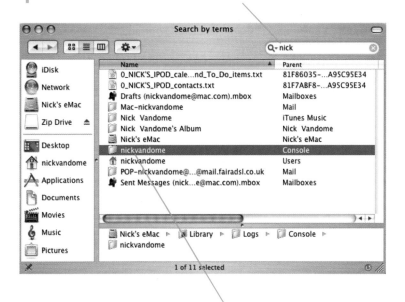

2 The search results are shown here. Click on an item to see further details or double-click on it to open the item

## Advanced search

A more advanced search facility can be accessed by selecting File> Find from the Finder Menu bar:

Enter search criteria
here and click Search

# Creating aliases

Aliases are shortcuts to the actual version of items. This can include programs, folders and files. Aliases take up virtually no disk space and numerous aliases can be created for a single item and then placed in various locations for ease of access. To create an alias:

1 Select an item in any open window, by clicking on it once

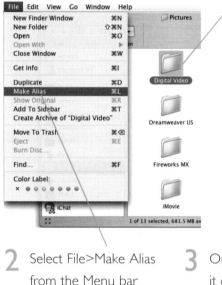

2 Select File>Make Alias from the Menu bar

3 Once an alias has been created, it can then be moved to the required location (in this case the Documents folder)

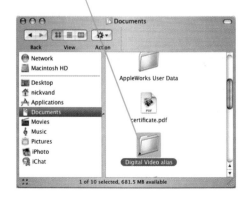

# Copying and moving items

Items can be copied and moved within OS X by using the copy and paste method or by dragging:

## Copy and paste

1 Select an item and select Edit>Copy from the Menu bar

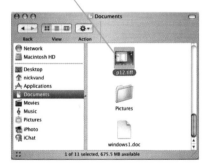

*When an item is copied, it is placed on the Clipboard and remains there until another item is copied.*

2 Move to the target location and select Edit>Paste item from the Menu bar. The item is then pasted into the new location

## Dragging

*Hold down the Option key while dragging to copy an item rather than moving it.*

Drag a file from one location into another to move it to that location

Pictures

# Working with windows

OS X has a much better method of managing open windows than any of the previous Apple operating systems. Whenever a new item is accessed from within the Finder, it replaces the existing window, rather than opening a new window. This means that the screen does not become cluttered with a lot of open windows. The exception to this is programs, which always open in a new window.

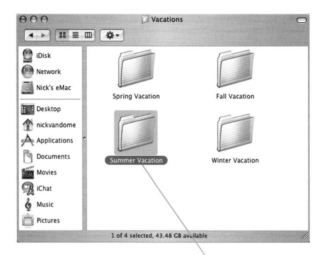

*Use the Back button to move back to the most recently accessed window.*

From within the Finder, if you select a new item (except a program) it replaces the existing item, rather than opening in a new window

## Program windows

As mentioned on the previous page, individual programs open up in new windows. However, it is still possible to move quickly between all open programs:

1 The currently active program is shown at the top of the open windows

2 All other windows are shown behind the active program window

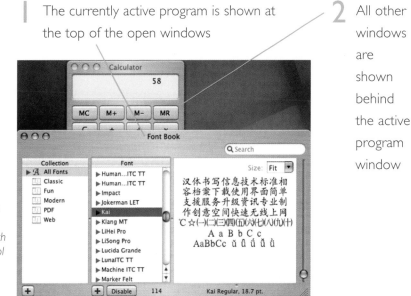

3 Click a window to bring it to the front and make it active

# Working with folders

When OS X is first installed, there are various folders that have already been created to hold programs and files. Some of these are essential (i.e. those containing programs) while others are created as an aid for where you might want to store the files that you create (such as the Pictures and Movies folders). Once you start working with OS X you will probably want to create your own folders, in which to store and organize your documents. This can be done on the desktop or within any level of your existing folder structure. To create a new folder:

Access the location in which you want to create the new folder (i.e. your Home folder) and select File>New Folder from the Menu bar

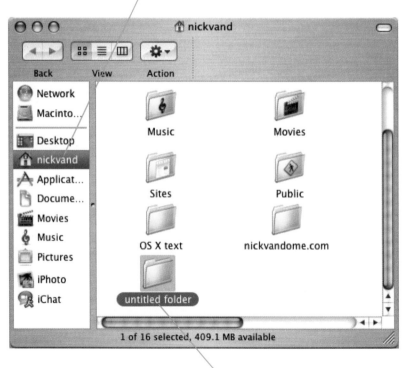

*Folders are always denoted by a folder icon. This is the same regardless of the Finder view which is selected. The only difference is that the icon is larger in Icon view than in List or Column views.*

2 A new, empty, folder is inserted at the selected location

3 Overtype the file name with a new one. Press Enter

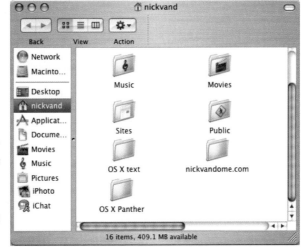

*You can create as many "nested" folders (i.e. folders within other folders) as you want. However, this makes your folder structure more complicated and, after time, you may forget where all your folders are and what they contain.*

4 Double-click on a folder to view its contents (at this point it should be empty)

*Content can be added to an empty folder by dragging it from another folder.*

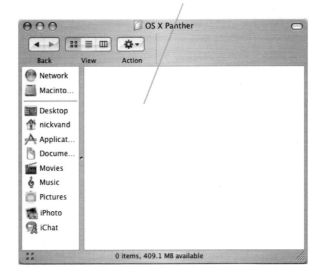

# Spring-loaded folders

Another method for moving items with the Finder is to use the spring-loaded folder option. This enables you to drag items into a folder but view the contents of the folder before you drop the items into it. This means that you can drag items into nested folders in a single operation. To do this:

*The spring-loaded folder technique can be used to move items between different locations within the Finder e.g. for moving files from your Pictures folder into your Home folder.*

1 Select the item you want to move

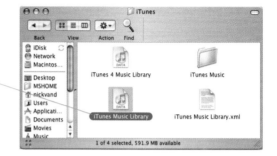

2 Drag the selected item over the folder into which you want to place it. Keep the mouse button held down

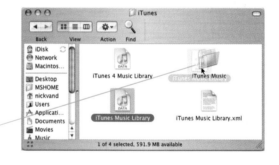

*Do not release the mouse button until you have reached the location into which you want to place the selected item.*

3 The folder will open, revealing its contents. The selected item can either be dropped into the folder or, if there are sub-folders, the same operation can be repeated until you find the folder into which you want to place the selected item

# Selecting items

Items within OS X folders can be selected by a variety of methods:

### Selecting by dragging
Drag the cursor to encompass the items to be selected. The selected items will become highlighted.

*Once items have been selected, a single command can be applied to all of them. For instance, you can copy a group of items by selecting them and then applying the Copy command from the Menu bar.*

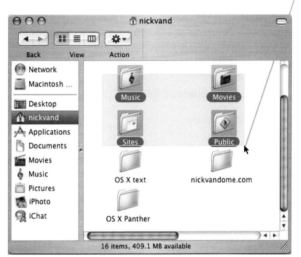

### Selecting by clicking
Click once on an item to select it, hold down Shift and then click on another item in a list to select a consecutive group of items.

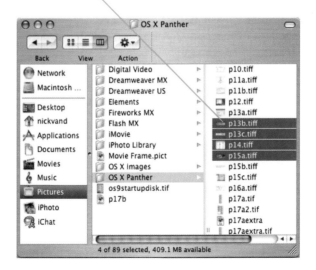

To select a non-consecutive group, select the first item by clicking on it once, then hold down the Command key (the one with the Apple symbol on it) and select the other required items. The selected items will appear highlighted.

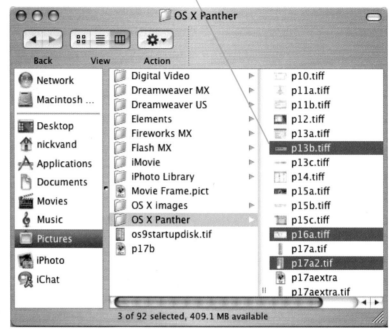

*The Select All command selects all of the elements within the active item. For instance, if the active item is a word processing document, the Select All command will select all of the items within the document; if it is a folder it will select all of the items within that folder.*

## Select All

To select all of the items in a folder, select Edit>Select All from the Menu bar:

# Labelling items

With the Finder it is possible to label items (including files, folders and programs) so that they can easily be identified for specific purposes. This could be for items that were created on a certain date or to quickly identify a particular type of document. To do this:

*Labels are visible regardless of the View option that is selected in the Finder.*

1 Select an item, or group of items, to which you want to apply labels

2 Click the Actions button and select a color for the label, or labels

3 The colored labels are applied to the selected items. Other items can then have other label colors applied to them

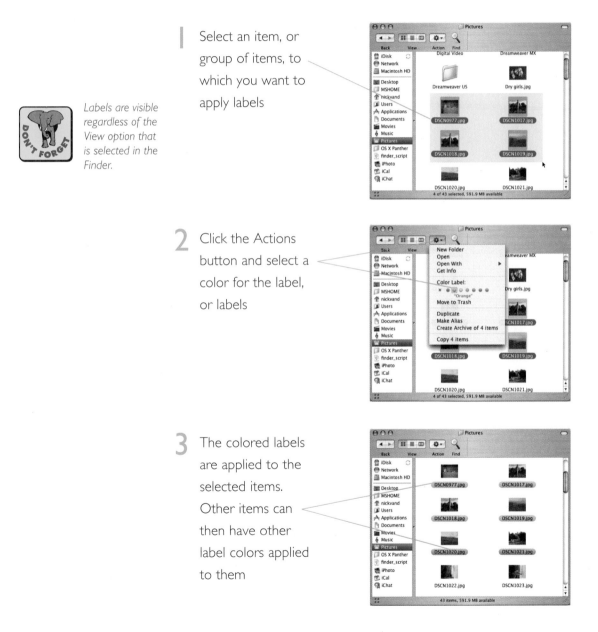

# Menus

The main Apple menu bar in OS X contains a variety of menus, which are consistent regardless of the program in operation:

**    Finder   File   Edit   View   Go   Window   Help**

- Apple menu. This is denoted by a translucent blue apple and contains general information about the computer, a preferences option for changing the functionality and appearance of the Dock and options for closing down the computer

- Finder menu. This contains a preferences option for amending the functionality and appearance of the Finder and also options for emptying the Trash and accessing other programs (under the Services option)

- File menu. This contains common commands for working with open documents,  such as opening and closing files, creating aliases, moving to the Trash, ejecting external devices and burning discs

- Edit menu. This contains common commands that apply to the majority of programs used on the Mac. These include undo, cut, copy, paste, select all and show the contents of the clipboard i.e. items that have been cut or copied

- View. This contains options for how windows and folders are displayed within the Finder and for customizing the Finder toolbar

- Go. This can be used to navigate around your computer. This includes moving to your Home folder, your iDisk, your Applications folder, recently opened items and also remote servers for connecting to other computers on a network

- Window. This contains commands to organize the currently open programs and files on your desktop

- Help. This contains the Mac Help files which contain information about all aspects of OS X

# iLife

The term iLife refers to the programs that are bundled with OS X and which form the foundation of Apple's "digital hub" strategy. This is designed to make every aspect of digital life as easy and as user-friendly as possible. The iLife group of programs cover the areas of digital images, music (listening to and creating), video and DVDs. This chapter looks at each of these programs and shows how they can be used to enhance a digital lifestyle.

## Covers

Chapter Four

# iPhoto

iPhoto is the image management program for OS X. The intention of iPhoto is to make the organizing, manipulation and sharing of digital images as easy as possible. To begin using iPhoto:

Click once on this icon on the Dock

*The Photo Library is where all downloaded images are displayed. If new albums are created and images placed into them, the images are visible in the album but they are, in effect, just a reference back to the images in the Photo Library. The means that images can be included in numerous albums without having to make several copies: each occurrence is a reference back to the Photo Library.*

2 Connect your digital camera to your Mac via either USB or FireWire. The connected camera is displayed here

3 Click here to import the images from the camera. These are then displayed in the Photo Library, which contains all of the photos in iPhoto

## Viewing images

Click here to view images in different albums

*iPhoto downloads all of the images held on a camera's memory card; there is no facility to select specific images before downloading.*

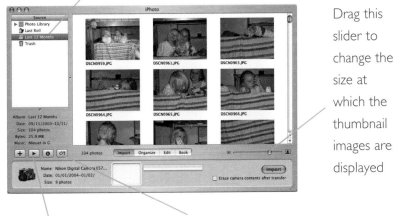

Drag this slider to change the size at which the thumbnail images are displayed

*Check on the "Erase camera contents after transfer" check box if you want images to be removed from your camera's memory card once they have been downloaded by iPhoto.*

Click here to view the images as a slideshow

Select an image and click here to change its orientation

## Organizing images

Select an image and click here to enter a new name for it

*The first time that you download images with iPhoto, the images in the Photo Library and the Last Roll folder will be the same.*

Click here to access the organizing options

## Creating albums

New albums can be created to store images from a particular event or time period. Images in new albums refer back to the originals in the Photo Library, so any changes to these originals will be reflected in the individual albums too. To create new albums:

*If you delete an image from the Photo Library it will also be deleted from any other albums in which it appears. This is because each image in an album is only a reference back to the master image stored in the Photo Library.*

1 Click here to create a new album

2 Enter the name for the new album and click OK

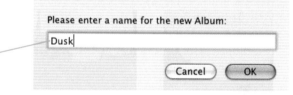

*Multiple images can be selected by dragging around them with the cursor.*

3 Select all of the images to be placed in the new album and drag them into it

## Editing

Although iPhoto is not a fully-featured image editing program, some basic editing functions can be performed, including adjusting the brightness and contrast, cropping and removing red-eye:

Click here to access the editing functions

Click here to make an image black and white or sepia

*The Enhance button has to be selected before the brightness and contrast can be corrected.*

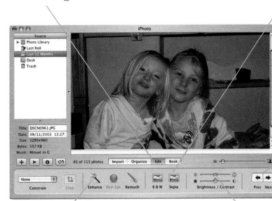

Click here to access Next and Previous images

*The Retouch tool can be used to remove small blemishes from an image. To do this, select the tool and drag over the required area on the image. The effected area will then be blended into the surrounding area.*

Click here to access color correction controls

Drag these sliders to change the brightness and contrast of an image

For cropping an image or for selecting an area for removing red-eye, first drag on the image to select the required area

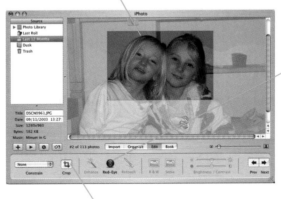

*Red-eye is removed automatically, there is no need to change the color manually. For removing red-eye, zoom in around the effected area only.*

Click here to remove red-eye from the selected area

Click here to crop the selected area

## Publishing and sharing

iPhoto has options for publishing and sharing images in a number of different ways. These are located in the Organize section, which is accessed by clicking on the Organize button:

Click here to print a selected image

Click here to view the current album as a slideshow

Click here to email images

Click here to burn the selected images onto a disk

*The Book section within iPhoto provides the option for ordering a completed booklet of the selected photos. This is an online service and there are options for specifying the appearance and style of the booklet.*

*See Chapter Seven for details of the .Mac online services, including creating Web pages with HomePage.*

Click here to order prints, or a book, online

Click here to display images as a Web page or a slideshow within the .Mac online service

Click here to set an image as your desktop

Click here to export images to the iDVD program

# iTunes

iTunes is Apple's jukebox software that allows CDs to be played and copied onto a computer. It also allows for the burning of music onto CDs, provides access to numerous online radio stations and is an entry point to the Apple Music Store which can be used to buy music online legally. It also works seamlessly with the iPod portable music player.

## Playing a CD

*To open iTunes, click on this icon on the Dock:*

2 Select an item and click on the Play button to start a track

1 Insert a CD. The contents are displayed here

*If you are copying CDs with OS X, make sure that you do not use copyrighted material as this is illegal.*

| ▲ | Song Name | Time | Artist | Album | Genre |
|---|---|---|---|---|---|
| 1 | ☑ Track 01 | 14:17 | | | |
| 2 | ☑ Track 02 | 9:37 | | | |
| 3 | ☑ Track 03 | 5:14 | | | |
| 4 | ☑ Track 04 | 17:28 | | | |

**Source:** Library, Radio, Music Store, Audio CD, 60's Music, My Top Rated, Recently Played, Top 25 Most Played

4 songs, 46.6 minutes, 470.8 MB

*Record companies are currently producing copy-protected CDs that cannot be copied on computers. These types of CDs can cause problems if they are played on Macs.*

Shuffle the tracks so they play in a random order

Repeat the current list, or single song if only one is selected

Graphic equalizer

Visual effects. This produces a psychedelic effect while the music is playing

Eject. This ejects the current CD

### Playlists

With iTunes you can create playlists of your favorite tracks from
different CDs. To do this you have to highlight songs in the
Library then add them to a Playlist. To do this:

1 Insert an audio CD and check on the boxes next to the items
you want to add to the Library

*By default, songs
are imported in
the AAC format.
This is an audio
file format that
uses high levels of compression
while still retaining good sound
quality. iTunes also supports
downloading in MP3, AIFF and
WAV formats. Select iTunes>
Preferences from the Menu bar
and click on the Importing tab to
see all of the options for
importing from a CD.*

2 Click on
the Import
button

4 Give the Playlist a name

*You can access
names for CD
tracks by selecting
Advanced>Get
CD Track Names
from the Menu bar. However,
this requires a connection to the
Internet.*

3 Click on
the Add
Playlist
button

5 Double-click on the Library and drag and
drop items from it into the Playlist

## iTunes and the iPod

The iPod is Apple's portable music player and it is one of the great commercial successes of the digital age. It works seamlessly with iTunes so that your entire music library can be transferred onto your iPod. Also, whenever the iPod is connected to your Mac, via a FireWire cable, recently added music is synchronized on the iPod. In addition to music, iPods can also be used to store Address Book and Calendar details. To use an iPod with iTunes

*Music cannot be copied back from an iPod into iTunes.*

*iPods can also be updated automatically by clicking on the iPod icon in iSync and selecting the first two options, "Turn on iPod synchronization" and "Automatically synchronize when iPod is connected". For more information on iSync, see Chapter Five.*

1 The connected iPod is shown here

2 Select File>Update Songs on iPod from the Menu bar

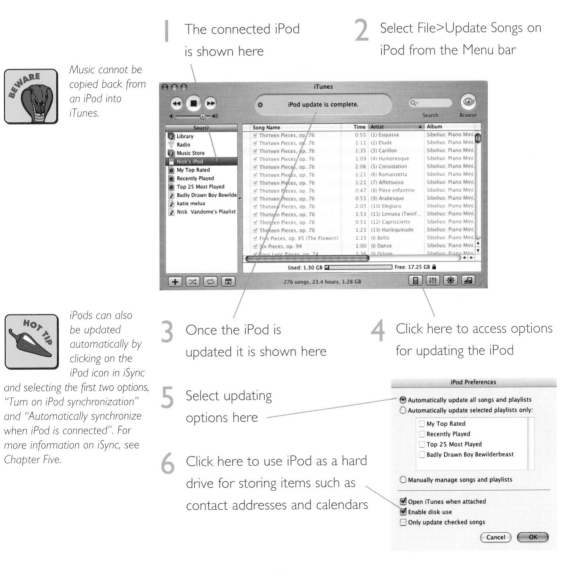

3 Once the iPod is updated it is shown here

4 Click here to access options for updating the iPod

5 Select updating options here

6 Click here to use iPod as a hard drive for storing items such as contact addresses and calendars

## iTunes Music Store

To further enhance iTunes and the iPod there is now an online iTunes Music Store that can be used to download legally a wide variety of music. To use the Music Store:

*The Music Store is not available in all countries and you have to register before you can start downloading music from it.*

1 Click here to access the Music Store

2 Click here to access the available types of music

*Blank CDs come in two main formats, recordable ones (CD-R) and re-recordable ones (CD-RW). The recordable ones can only be recorded on once but re-recordable ones can be copied over numerous times. Because of this, re-recordable ones are more expensive.*

## Disk burning

Once you have downloaded music into iTunes you will be able to burn it onto a blank CD or DVD. To do this:

1 Copy the required items into a playlist and select the playlist

*CDs created from the AAC format can be played on commercial CD players.*

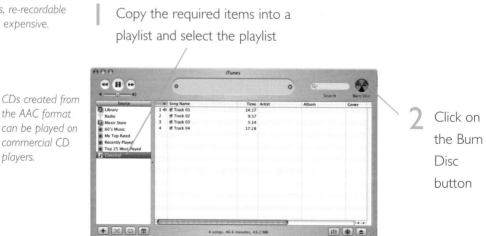

2 Click on the Burn Disc button

# iMovie

*To open iMovie, click on this icon on the Dock:*

iMovie is Apple's video editing program that can be used to edit video from a digital video camera or video that has been converted from an analog camera. Once video has been obtained, it can be edited in the same way, regardless of its original source. The first step in the process is to obtain video which can be used in iMovie.

## Obtaining video from a video camera

1 Attach the video camera to your Mac computer. (This involves connecting it via the FireWire connection.)

Drag this slider to the left

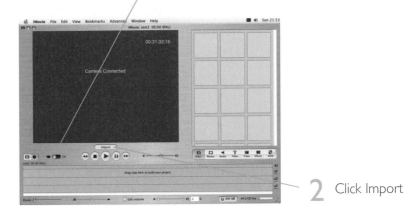

2 Click Import

*Make sure you have a FireWire connection on your computer before you start working with digital video. This is used for downloading the video onto your computer and it works very quickly, which is essential for digital video and its large file sizes.*

3 Video clips are downloaded here, in the Clip Pane

4 Drag this slider to the right to enter edit mode

## Adding clips

Once video clips have been downloaded they can be assembled into a project in iMovie. This is done by adding the clips to the timeline or storyboard. After this, other editing techniques can be applied, such as transitions and video effects. It is also possible to edit the video clips, to get rid of any unwanted footage.

1 Drag clips from the clip pane to the storyboard or timeline

2 Click here to preview the selected clip

*The order in which clips are played can be edited by dragging the clips in front of, or behind, each other.*

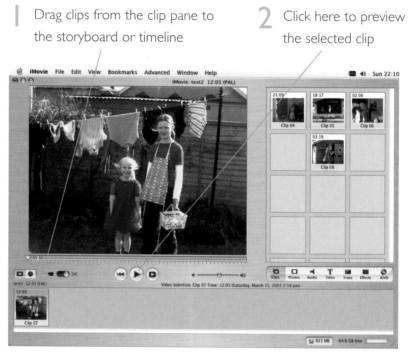

*Timeline is a phrase that is used frequently in the world of video and animation. It refers to the entire duration of a clip and its elements. The storyboard displays each video clip as a thumbnail image.*

3 Click here to toggle between timeline and storyboard modes

## Trimming clips

To remove unwanted footage at the beginning or end of a clip:

*The playhead is the line that moves along a video clip in the clip viewer or on the timeline.*

1 Drag this marker to the point at which you want the clip to begin or end

2 Select Edit> Clear from the Menu bar

## Cropping clips

To save specific footage in a clip:

*Clips can be split in two so that they can be edited independently of one another. To do this, drag the playhead to the point at which you want to split the clip and select Edit>Split Video Clip at Playhead from the Menu bar. To restore a clip that has been split, select Advanced>Restore Clip from the Menu bar. This restores the clip to its original format, regardless of how many times it has been split.*

1 Drag these markers to the points of the clip you want to retain

2 Select Edit>Crop from the Menu bar

## Adding audio

Audio can be included from a variety of sources: the audio recorded with the video footage (synchronous), sound effects and background music or narration. To include audio:

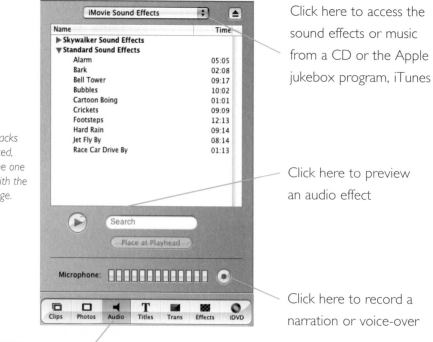

Click here to access the sound effects or music from a CD or the Apple jukebox program, iTunes

Click here to preview an audio effect

Click here to record a narration or voice-over

*All audio tracks can be edited, including the one recorded with the video footage.*

*Audio tracks can be edited by clicking on the track and dragging the button that subsequently appears.*

Click here to access the audio options

Drag an effect onto the timeline at the point you want it to play

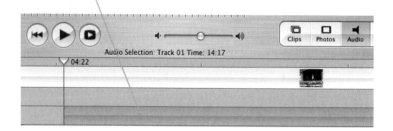

## Adding titles

Textual titles can be added to any scene within a movie. This could be used as an introductory title, closing credits or for a form of textual commentary throughout a movie. To add titles:

*Titles can be added throughout a movie, not just at the beginning or the end. They can be used as subtitles during a movie to explain what is happening or being said.*

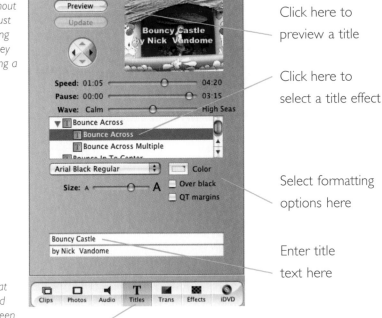

Click here to preview a title

Click here to select a title effect

Select formatting options here

Enter title text here

*Make sure that there is a good contrast between the text color of your titles and the background of the clip on which they appear.*

Click here to access the titles options

Drag a title onto the timeline in front of the clip you want it to appear, even if the Over Black option has been selected

*To add a title, you drag the title effect name onto the timeline, rather than the text for the title.*

## Adding transitions

Any good movie needs smooth transitions from one scene to another and iMovie provides various options for achieving this with your own movies:

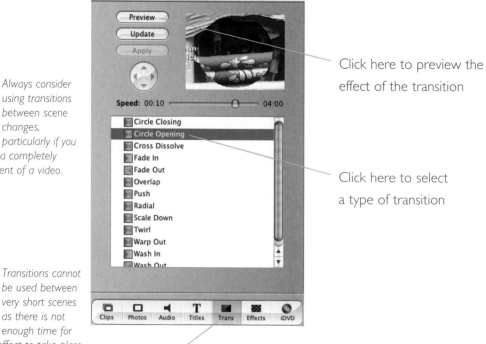

Click here to preview the effect of the transition

Click here to select a type of transition

*Always consider using transitions between scene changes, particularly if you are moving to a completely different segment of a video.*

*Transitions cannot be used between very short scenes as there is not enough time for the transition effect to take place before the scene has ended.*

Click here to access the transitions options

To apply a transition, drag it between the two scenes you want it to apply

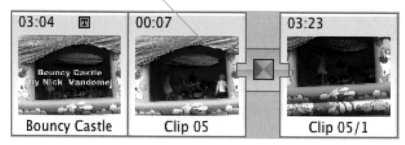

*Select Storyboard view to see a quick overview of all of the transitions in an iMovie project.*

## Adding effects

iMovie provides options for adding different effects, which can be applied to scenes within movies. These effects include making a scene black and white or adding a sepia tone:

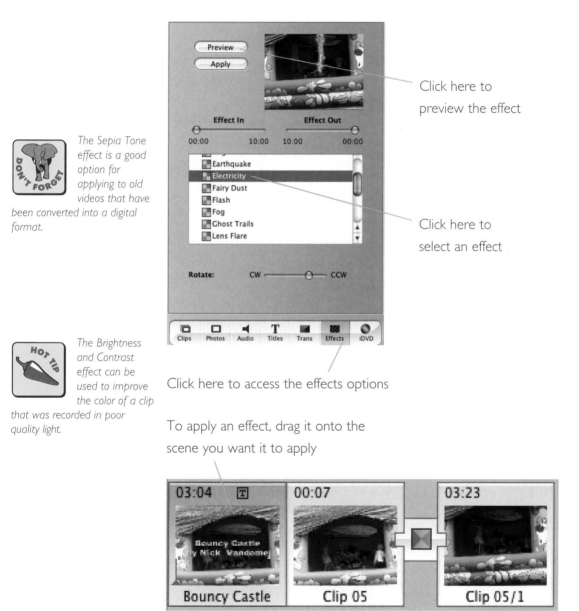

*The Sepia Tone effect is a good option for applying to old videos that have been converted into a digital format.*

*The Brightness and Contrast effect can be used to improve the color of a clip that was recorded in poor quality light.*

Click here to preview the effect

Click here to select an effect

Click here to access the effects options

To apply an effect, drag it onto the scene you want it to apply

## Adding chapter markers

Once a movie is completed, each clip can have chapter markers inserted into them. These can subsequently be used when creating menus for the movie in iDVD. To add chapter markers:

*Once chapter markers have been added, these will be detected automatically by iDVD. This will mark the video at different sections, each of which can be accessed independently from any DVD that is then created.*

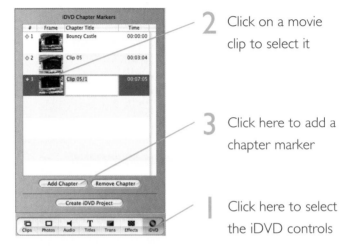

2 Click on a movie clip to select it

3 Click here to add a chapter marker

| Click here to select the iDVD controls

## Sharing video

Once a movie has been completed it can either be saved as an iMovie project or it can be exported into a different format. To do this:

*Different video formats use differing methods of compression when the File>Share command is selected. Videos that will be used on the Web have the greatest amount of compression applied to them, while those to be used for DVDs have the least amount of compression applied to them.*

| Select File>Share from the Menu bar

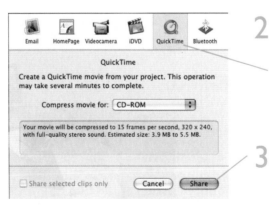

2 Click here to select an option for sharing the movie. Each option creates the movie in a different format

3 Click Share

# iDVD

*To open iDVD, click on this icon on the Dock:*

iDVD is a program for creating and burning professional-looking DVDs. It works most effectively with iMovie files and it can be used to add menus, titles and buttons to movies to improve their appearance and increase their functionality. The menus created with iDVD are similar in the way they look and operate to those on commercial DVDs. Menus can be used to link to different movies or they can link to different points (chapters) within a single movie. The main components of iDVD are:

*If you do not have a SuperDrive connected to your Mac, you will not be able to install the iDVD software.*

*The final DVD should only be created (burned) when all of the elements have been added within iDVD.*

Background          Titles          Play whole movie button

Image or movie clip

View scenes within a movie button (these are available if a movie has had chapter markers added)

iDVD controls

## Creating menus

Menus are a part of a DVD that appear when it is first played. They give the user the opportunity to select which movie, or part of a movie, they want to watch. To create a menu in iDVD you need the graphical interface, buttons linking to the movie, or movies, and the movie files themselves. To do this:

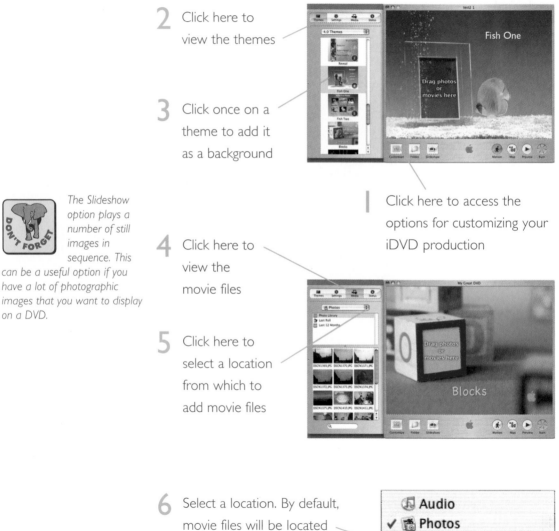

2 Click here to view the themes

3 Click once on a theme to add it as a background

1 Click here to access the options for customizing your iDVD production

*The Slideshow option plays a number of still images in sequence. This can be a useful option if you have a lot of photographic images that you want to display on a DVD.*

4 Click here to view the movie files

5 Click here to select a location from which to add movie files

6 Select a location. By default, movie files will be located in the Movies folder

*You do not have to use the default name for movie clips, as you can edit the title once it has been added.*

**7** Add movie files by dragging them here. By default their title is that of the original file name

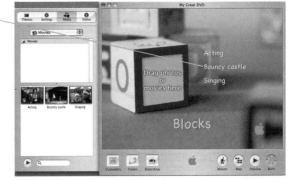

*Text blocks can be edited by selecting the text in them and then overtyping with new text.*

**8** Add a movie clip or a photograph here by dragging it from the relevant folder

*Background music can also be added to a menu, by dragging an audio file onto the menu from the Media panel.*

**9** Click on a text block and click here to select formatting options for the text

## File structure

If you are working with numerous video clips and menus within the same DVD it can become confusing trying to remember where all of the different elements are placed in relation to each other. To simplify matters, the overall structure of the DVD can be viewed using the Map option:

*Autoplay items are those that play automatically when the DVD is activated in a DVD player. This can be in the form of a still image or a short, introductory video clip. Once it has played the main menu becomes available.*

Autoplay items

DVD menus. Main and sub menus can be displayed

DVD content i.e. video files or still images

Click here to view the file structure of the DVD

## Testing menus

Since burning a DVD can be a time-consuming operation (and more expensive than burning a CD) it is best to thoroughly test the functionality of the menu before you commit it to disk. To do this:

*Although it can be time-consuming, it is worth check all of the movies in your iDVD project as well as the menu functionality, just in case there are any mistakes that you want to edit.*

Use these controls to test the functionality of the DVD menu

Click here to preview the DVD menu

## Burning a DVD

Once you have added all of the content, themes and menus with iDVD, you can burn it onto a DVD. This can be played back on a computer with a DVD drive or on most commercially available DVD players. To do this:

*Burning DVDs is a slow process, so it is best to have something else to do while iDVD is burning your files onto a DVD.*

1 Insert a DVD into the SuperDrive. (If no disk is inserted the following warning dialog box appears)

*iDVD uses the DVD-R format of disk for burning DVDs.*

*At present, there is no standardization in recordable DVD formats. Different companies have their own preferred options in terms of format and, as yet, no clearly favored option has emerged. Although most recordable DVDs should play on standard DVD players, not all DVDs will work on different computers.*

2 Click on the Burn button. This can be accessed at any time from within iDVD

# GarageBand

GarageBand is the latest addition to the iLife suite. It is a music authoring program that can be used to create music from either computerized tracks or real instruments. Once the basic tracks have been recorded they can be mixed together or have special effects added to them.

## Getting started with GarageBand

*By default, GarageBand files are saved in the GarageBand format which has a .band extension.*

1 Click once on this icon on the Dock

*GarageBand files are much smaller in size when they are saved in the GarageBand format than when they are exported into another format, e.g. for use in iTunes.*

2 Enter details for the new project and click Create

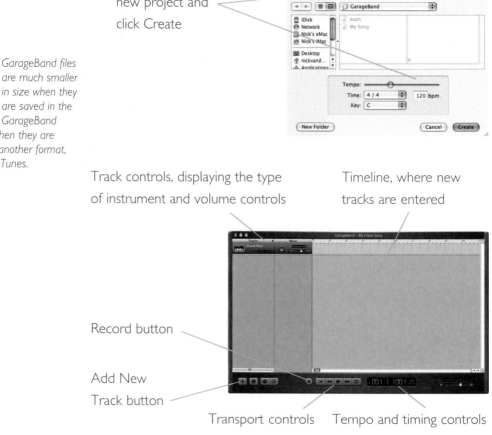

Track controls, displaying the type of instrument and volume controls

Timeline, where new tracks are entered

Record button

Add New Track button

Transport controls

Tempo and timing controls

3 Select either a Real or
a Software instrument
and click OK

*If you want to use
a real instrument,
such as a guitar,
make sure it has
an attachment,
such as a USB cable, to connect
it to your computer.*

4 A new track is created with the appropriate instrument. Use the
Mixer to alter the volume of the track

*The playhead is
the red line that
moves along a
track as it is
being played or
recorded. Wherever the playhead
is, that is what is heard at that
point.*

5 Select Window>Keyboard from the Menu bar (the keyboard is
used as the input device for all software instruments)

6 Click here
to start
recording

7 Click on the keyboard to
record individual notes

8 As the notes are played, they are
recorded on the track on the timeline

## Recording vocals

Vocals are treated as a real instrument in GarageBand and both of these elements are added in a similar way. To add vocals there has to be a compatible microphone attached to your Mac. To add vocals:

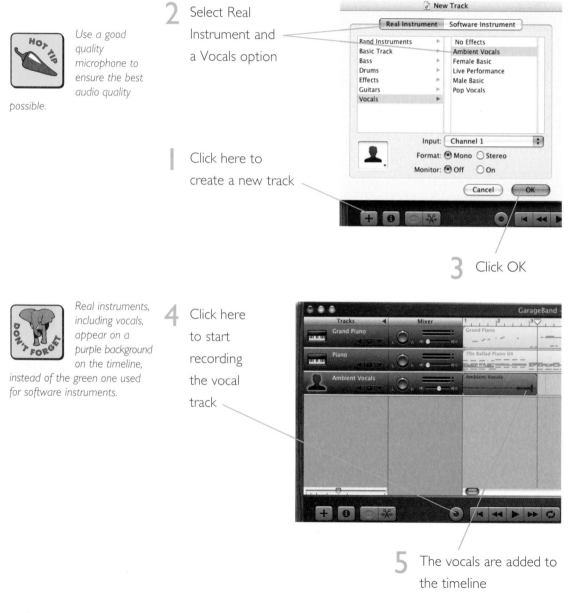

**HOT TIP**

*Use a good quality microphone to ensure the best audio quality possible.*

2 Select Real Instrument and a Vocals option

1 Click here to create a new track

3 Click OK

**DON'T FORGET**

*Real instruments, including vocals, appear on a purple background on the timeline, instead of the green one used for software instruments.*

4 Click here to start recording the vocal track

5 The vocals are added to the timeline

## Using loops

Loops are prerecorded segments of music that can be added to songs as backgrounds or used to create whole songs. To use loops:

Most pieces of looped music are fairly short initially. However, it is possible to extend them so they continue for a whole song, if required. See next page for details.

| Click here to access the loops window

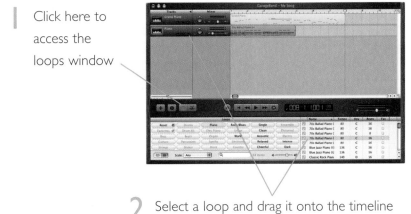

2 Select a loop and drag it onto the timeline

## Editing tracks

Areas within a track are known as regions and these can be edited independently from the rest of the song. To do this:

| Click here to access the editing window

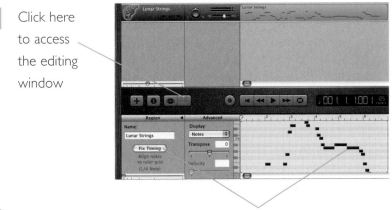

2 The region can be edited by applying a fixed timing or individual notes can be selected and edited by moving them or lengthening them in the editing window

### Extending regions

When using segments of music, particularly loops, an effective technique is to repeat part or all of a region. This can be done by extending the length of a region. To do this:

*Regions can be copied, by clicking on them and selecting Edit> Copy from the Menu bar. They can then be pasted into another part of the track by selecting Edit>Paste from the Menu bar.*

Move the cursor over the end of a region until a circular arrowhead appears. Use this to extend the region by dragging. The extended region is denoted by a small v shape on the timeline

*Regions can be moved within a track by dragging them to the desired position.*

### Exporting songs

Once a song has been completed it can be saved, burned onto a disk or exported into iTunes. This enables it to be played on your Mac and it can also be exported to an iPod via iTunes. To export songs to iTunes, first open it in GarageBand, then:

1 Select File>Export to iTunes from the Menu bar

*GarageBand files are exported to iTunes in the .aif format. These cannot then be opened by GarageBand. If you want to edit the file again, open up the original GarageBand file.*

2 Open iTunes. The exported song will be available in the Library

# Getting productive with OS X

In addition to the iLife suite of programs, there are several other applications within OS X Panther that can be used to create, store and display information. This chapter shows how to access and use these programs, so that you can get the most out of OS X Panther and your Mac.

## Covers

Chapter Five

# Address Book

*To open the Address Book, click on this icon on the Dock or in the Applications folder.*

In previous versions of OS X, the Address Book was incorporated into the email program. However, in Panther it has been liberated and exists as an independent program that resides within the Applications folder. The Address Book can be used to store contact information, which can then be used in different applications and even published on the Web so that you can access it from computers around the world. The Address Book can be opened by double-clicking on the Address Book icon in the Applications folder in the Finder.

## Overview

The Address Book contains contact information, either for groups or for individuals. The Address Book can display this information in two ways:

*Address Book can import contacts in the vCard format (which uses the .vcf extension). So if you have a lot of contacts on a Windows-based PC you can export them as vCards, copy them onto a disk and import them into Address Book. To do this, select File>Import>vCards from the Menu bar and browse to the folder on the disk on which they are held.*

1  Click here to view card and column information

2  Click here to view card information only i.e. individual Address Book entries

## Adding contact information

The main function of the Address Book is to include details of personal and business contacts. This has to be done manually for each entry, but it can prove to be a valuable resource once it has been completed. To add contact information:

*Different types of entries have different icons next to them. The entry for the computer's administrator is a black silhouette rather than an index card used for a standard entry.*

1 Click here to add a new contact

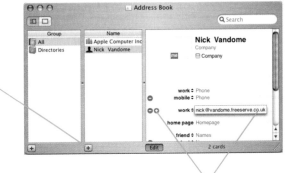

2 Click on a category and enter contact information. Press Tab to move to the next field. Click the green button to access additional options for a certain category

3 Click here and browse your hard drive to add a photograph for the selected contact

4 Contact information is shown here

## Adding personal contacts

Create a new contact and enter the information here. Make sure the Company box is checked off

*The search box can be used to quickly find specific entries of groups of contacts with a shared characteristic.*

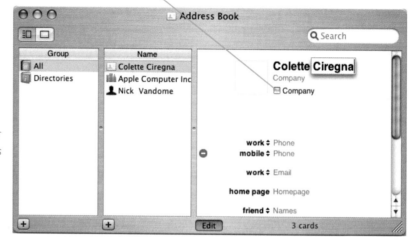

## Adding business contacts

Create a new contact and check on the Company box. Business contacts and personal contacts have different icons

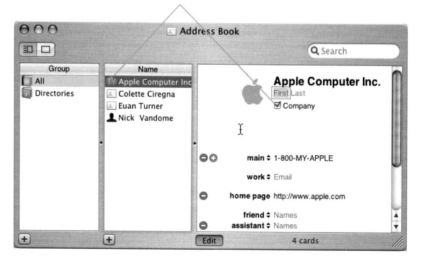

...cont'd

## Creating groups

In addition to creating individual entries in the Address Book, group contacts can also be created. This is a way of grouping contacts with similar interests. Once a group has been created, all of the entries within it can be accessed and contacted by selecting the relevant entry under the Group column. To create a group:

1 Click here to create a new group. Type a name for the group

2 Drag existing contacts into the new group

3 Click on a group to view its contents

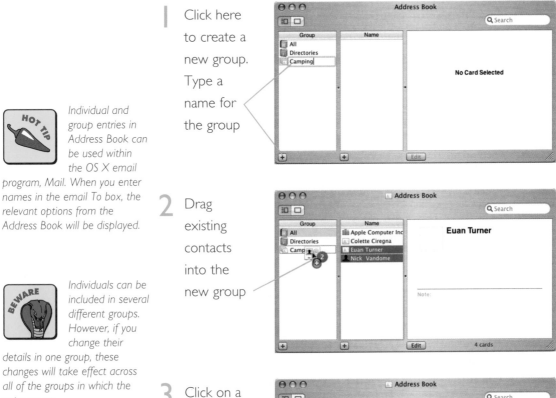

*Individual and group entries in Address Book can be used within the OS X email program, Mail. When you enter names in the email To box, the relevant options from the Address Book will be displayed.*

*Individuals can be included in several different groups. However, if you change their details in one group, these changes will take effect across all of the groups in which the entry occurs.*

# iCal

*To open iCal, click on this icon on the Dock or in the Applications folder.*

iCal is a calendar and organizer that can be used to keep track of all your social and business appointments, important dates and To Do lists. Calendars can be created for different categories and they can even be published on the Web via a personal account with the .Mac online service. To use iCal:

## Viewing iCal

Available calendars          Calendar content goes here

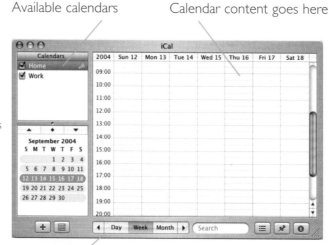

*When iCal is opened it displays the current date in the icon on the Dock.*

Viewing options          Click here to change the calendar view

*iCal calendars can be published online using the .Mac service. For more information on this, see Chapter Seven.*

## Adding calendar content

1 Click on an existing calendar

To create an all-
day appointment,
click on the "i"
icon at the
bottom right of
the iCal window. In the new
panel, check on the "all-day" box.

2 Click here to select a month

3 Drag on a day and enter
the required text

4 To determine
the look of the
calendar, select
iCal>Preferences
from the Menu
bar and select
the required
options

## Adding calendars

Numerous calendars can be created with iCal, so you can keep track of business appointments, social events and group activities. Each calendar is color-coded and multiple calendar information can be displayed within the calendar window. To add calendars:

1 Click here to create a new calendar and type a name for it in the Calendar window

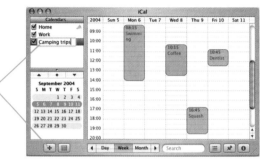

*Events can be moved by dragging them from the current location to a new one.*

2 Enter events for the new calendar. They will appear in the calendar's default color

3 All calendar events for a selected date are displayed. If events overlap, the details of the selected calendar appear above the other calendars

## To Do lists

Within iCal there is an option to add reminders via the To Do list. To do this:

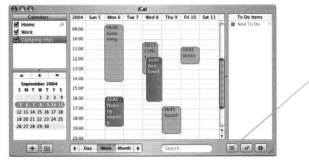

Select a calendar and click here to show the To Do list

2 Select File>New To Do from the Menu bar

3 Enter details for the To Do list. Select a different calendar to add reminders for items within it. These will appear in the designated color for the selected calendar

# iSync

iSync is a small program within OS X, but one which you may grow to love. Its role is to make sure that information within the Address Book, Calendar and, where applicable, iTunes are updated and synchronized on a variety of devices and locations. These include the .Mac service, the iPod, handheld computers and cellphones. With iSync you can be sure that you are always looking at your most up-to-date information, regardless of where you are or the type of device on which you are viewing the data. To use iSync:

1 Click on this icon on the Dock or in the Applications folder

2 Select Devices>Add Device from the Menu bar for each device to be included in the synchronization process

3 Click on a device to select preferences for the iSync process

*iPods can also be updated directly from within iTunes, without the need to synchronize all of the other items on your computer.*

**NICK'S IPOD**

Last synchronized: Thursday, 1 April 2004 15:42PM

☑ **Turn on NICK'S IPOD synchronization**

☑ **Automatically synchronize when iPod is connected**

☑ **Contacts** _____

       Synchronize: [ All contacts ▼ ]

☑ **Calendars** _____

       ◉ All
       ○ Selected: ☑ Home
                  ☑ Work

**...cont'd**

4 Click here to begin the iSync process

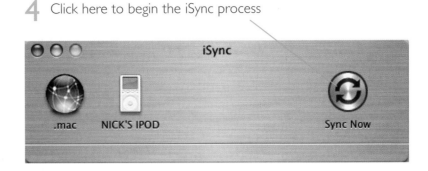

5 For some devices the update is shown within the relevant program

*If you are syncing with your .Mac service, you will need to have an active Internet connection.*

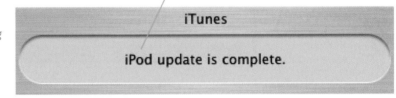

6 When syncing from your computer to the .Mac service for the first time, the following alert appears asking how you want the process to be handled. Once you are happy with the options, click on Sync

*If you are syncing with your .Mac service, make sure the synchronization is going the way you want. If you have less data on .Mac you probably do not want that to synchronize over the data on your computer.*

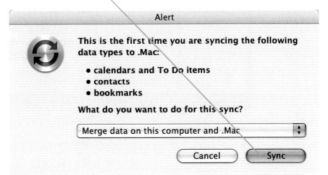

# Font Book

*To open the Font Book, click on this icon on the Dock or in the Applications folder.*

The Font Book is an application that can be used to add, organize and remove fonts within OS X. To use the Font Book:

## Viewing fonts

The available fonts on the system can be viewed via the Font Book:

Click on a Collection and a Font. An example is displayed here

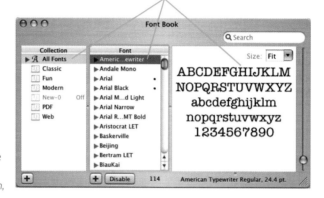

*Most computer users only use a small percentage of the fonts available to them, but it is best to keep most of them installed as you never know when you might want to use a different font.*

## Adding fonts

New fonts can be added through Font Book and existing fonts can be disabled throughout your computer. To do this.

*Fonts can be added from CDs, such as those found on the covers of computer magazines.*

1 Click here to add a new font

2 Click here to disable an existing font

# Preview

Preview is an OS X application that can be used to view multiple file types, particularly image file formats. This can be useful if you just want to view documents without editing them in a dedicated program, such as an image editing program. Preview can also be used to view PDF (Portable Document Format) files and also preview documents before they are printed. To use Preview:

1   Double-click on an item within the Finder

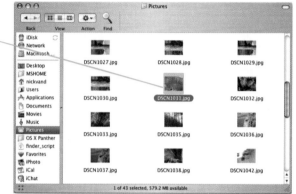

2   The selected file is displayed by Preview

# AppleWorks for OS X

AppleWorks is the Apple suite of productivity programs and it has been optimized to work effortlessly with the operating system. All iMac, iBook and eMac computers come with AppleWorks pre-installed and OS X ensures that its collection of programs work effectively and efficiently. The AppleWorks programs are:

- Word Processor

- Spreadsheet

*The version of AppleWorks for use with OS X is 6.2.4 or later.*

- Database

- Drawing

- Painting

- Presentation

Each of these applications function independently of the others, but it is possible to copy items from one program to another.

*AppleWorks documents can be saved into the equivalent Windows formats for transfer to a Windows-based PC. For instance, for a word processing document, select File>Save As from the AppleWorks Menu bar and select the required Word option under the File Format box.*

## Opening AppleWorks

AppleWorks is usually located within the Applications folder and can be opened as follows:

Open the AppleWorks folder and double-click here to launch the program

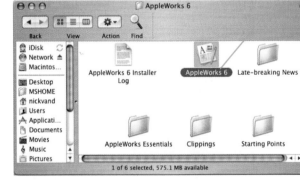

...cont'd

**2** Click here to select the standard applications

**3** Select the application you want to use. A brief description appears underneath the icon

*The Starting Points window can be accessed at any time within AppleWorks by selecting File>Show Starting Points from the Menu bar.*

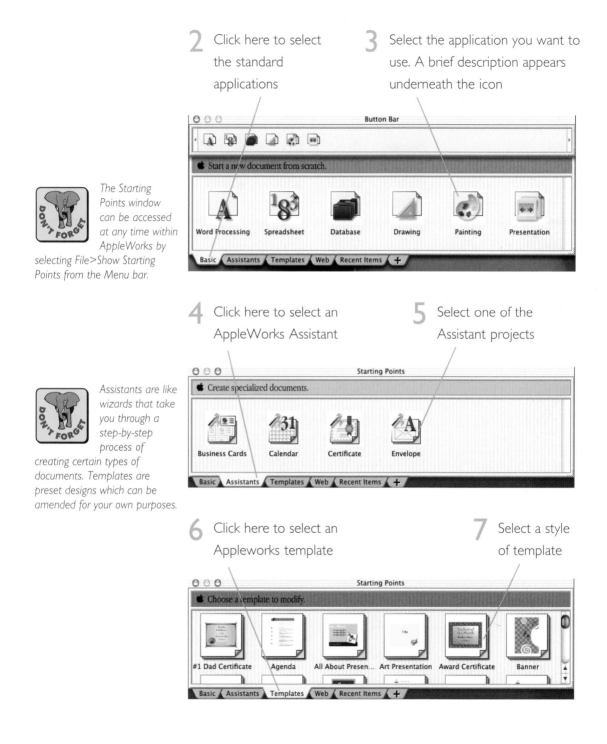

**4** Click here to select an AppleWorks Assistant

**5** Select one of the Assistant projects

*Assistants are like wizards that take you through a step-by-step process of creating certain types of documents. Templates are preset designs which can be amended for your own purposes.*

**6** Click here to select an Appleworks template

**7** Select a style of template

# OS X applications

There are several useful OS X programs in the Applications folder:

*As well as viewing PDF files, OS X can also create them without the need for an additional program. For more details on this, see page 109.*

Some of the applications (except those dealt with in this chapter) include:

*Image Capture can be used to download images from a digital device, unless you have set iPhoto to be the default for performing this task.*

- Acrobat Reader. A program that enables you to view PDF (Portable Document Format) files

- Calculator. A basic calculator

- Chess. Play online chess against your Mac computer

- Image Capture. A program for transferring images from a digital camera or scanner

- QuickTime Player. The default application for viewing video

- Internet Connect. Settings for connecting to the Internet

- iPhoto, iTunes, iMovie, iDVD and GarageBand. These are part of the iLife suite and covered in Chapter Four

- Safari. The OS X specific Web browser

- Internet Explorer. A browser for viewing Web pages

- Mail. The default email program

- Sherlock. The search facility for searching the Internet

- Stickies. A small program for adding note-like reminders

- TextEdit. A program for editing text files

# OS X utilities

In addition to the programs in the Applications folder, there are a number of utility programs that perform a variety of tasks within OS X. To access the Utilities:

1 Open the Applications folder and double-click on the Utilities folder

*The utilities are the workhorses of OS X. They do not have the glamour of programs such as iPhoto or iMovie but they perform vital information-gathering and general maintenance tasks.*

2 The available utilities are displayed within the Utilities folder

- Activity Monitor. This contains information about the system memory being used and disk activity

- AirPort Admin Utility. This can be used if you have an AirPort facility on your computer, which enables you to perform wireless networking

- AirPort Setup Assistant. This sets up the AirPort wireless networking facility

- Audio MIDI Setup. This can be used for adding audio devices and setting their properties

- Bluetooth File Exchange. This determines how files are exchanged between your computer and other Bluetooth devices (if this function is enabled)

- Bluetooth Serial Utility. Part of the Bluetooth wireless setup

- Bluetooth Setup Assistant. This can be used to set up a wireless Bluetooth network. To do this, you first have to have a USB Bluetooth module connected to your computer

- ColorSync Utility. This can be used to view and create color profiles on your computer. These can then be used by programs to try and match output color with the color that is displayed on the monitor

- Console. This displays the behind-the-scenes messages that are being passed around the computer while its usual tasks are being performed

- DigitalColor Meter. This can be used to measure the exact color values of a particular color

- Directory Access. This is an administration function for a network administrator. It enables them to give users access to various network services

- Disk Utility. This can be used to view information about attached disks and repair errors

*You may never need to use a utility like the Console, but it is worth having a look at just to see the inner workings of a computer.*

*The Grab utility is invaluable if you are producing manuals or books and need to display examples of a screen or program.*

- Grab. This is a utility which can be used to capture screen shots. These are images of the screen at a given point in time. You can grab different portions of the screen and even menus. The resultant images can be saved into different file formats

- Installer. This is used to install new programs and it works behind the scenes and launches automatically when you want to install a program

- Java folder. This is a folder that contains utilities that can be used to run and work with Java programs

- Keychain Access. This deals with items such as passwords when they are needed for networking

- NetInfo Manager. This is a utility that contains a database with information relating to all of the users of a particular computer. This includes details of different users, servers and general network details

- Network Utility. This is a Web utility that gathers information about different websites that have been visited

- ODBC Administrator. This can be used to work with databases that are ODBC (Object Database Connectivity) compliant. It can access multiple databases from a single application

*Stuffit Expander opens automatically when you try and open a file that has been compressed or encoded. It may also inform you that a newer version of Stuffit Expander is available to download. It is worth doing this so that you can process files that have been compressed and encoded with the latest version of the program.*

- Print Setup Utility. This is used to add and configure printers and to view the status of any current print jobs

- Stuffit Expander. This is used to decompress and decode other programs, usually ones that have been downloaded from the Web

- System Profiler. This contains details of the hardware devices and software applications that are installed on your computer

- Terminal. This is used as an entry point into the world of UNIX

# Printing

OS X Panther makes the printing process as simple as possible, partly by being able to automatically instal new printers as soon as they are connected to your Mac. However, it is also possible to instal printers manually. To do this:

*For most printers, OS X will detect them when they are first connected and they should be ready to use immediately without the need to instal any software or apply new settings.*

1 Open the Utilities folder within the Applications folder and double-click on the Printer Setup Utility

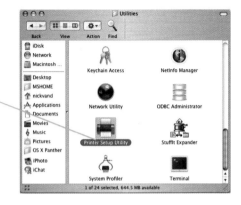

*To share a printer over a network, select the Sharing preference within System Preferences and check on Printer Sharing under Services. Then open the Printer Setup Utility and click the Add button. Select IP Printing from the first drop-down box. Then add the IP address of the computer connected to the printer, in the Printer Address box. (The IP address can be found at the bottom of the Sharing window when the Personal File Sharing option is checked on.) The printer should then be available to anyone connected to your network.*

2 Currently installed printers are displayed in the Printer List. Click here to add a new printer and follow the on-screen prompts

3 Once a printer has been installed (either automatically or manually) documents can be printed by selecting File>Print from the Menu bar. Print settings can be set at this point and they can also be set by selecting File>Page Setup from the Menu bar in most programs. Click OK to apply the required settings

# Creating PDF documents

PDF (Portable Document Format) is a file format that preserves the formatting of the original document and it can be viewed on a variety of computer platforms including Mac, Windows and UNIX. OS X Panther has a built-in PDF function that can produce PDF files from most programs. To do this:

*PDF files can be viewed in OS X with the Preview program or Adobe Acrobat Reader within the Applications folder.*

I Open a file in any program and select File>Print from the Menu bar. Then click here

2 Browse to a destination for the file and click Save

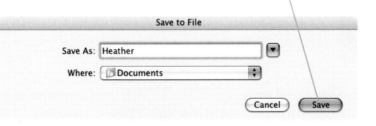

*PDF is an excellent option if you are creating documents such as instruction booklets or manuals.*

3 Look in the selected location to view the newly created PDF file

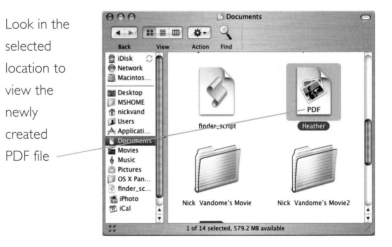

# Faxing documents

With OS X Panther you can fax any document as long as you have an internal or an external modem connected to your Mac. To do this:

1 Open the document you want to fax and select File>Print from the Menu bar

*You can set preferences for incoming faxes within the Print & Fax System preference under System Preferences. Here you can enter a number for incoming faxes, which will be received on your computer.*

2 In the Print dialog box, click the Fax button

| Printer: | Stylus Photo 750 | |
| Presets: | Standard | |
| | Copies & Pages | |

Copies: 1  ☑ Collated
Pages: ⦿ All
○ From: 1  to: 1

(?) (Preview) (Save As PDF...) (Fax....) (Cancel) (Print)

3 Enter a fax number and prefix in these boxes

4 Alternatively, click here to select a recipient from the Address Book

*If you select a recipient from the Address Book, make sure you have added the field for their fax number as this is the one that will be used in the To box of the Fax dialog box when a fax is sent.*

To: 123456

Subject: OS X Panther

Dialing Prefix: 0123  Modem: Internal Modem

Presets: Standard

Fax Cover Page

☑ Cover page

Amendments for Panther book

(?) (Preview)  (Cancel) (Fax)

5 Enter the rest of the details of the fax, including items to be displayed on the cover page. Click the Fax button to send

# Internet and email

The Internet is still one of the most rapidly developing areas of the digital world. This chapter shows how to get the most out of this vital resource. It shows various ways of connecting to the Internet and how to use the OS X Web browser, Safari, and its email program, Mail. It also covers text chatting and video conferencing over the Internet and then looks at the powerful search facility, Sherlock.

## Covers

**Chapter Six**

# Getting connected

OS X Panther is designed very much with the Internet in mind and there are various ways to connect to the Internet through an Internet Service Provider (ISP). Once you have registered with an ISP they will send you details of how to connect to their service. This will usually include items such as your username, password and telephone number to contact when accessing their service (if using a dial-up modem). The main ways of connecting to the Internet via an ISP are a dial-up modem on a standard telephone line, a DSL (Digital Subscriber Line) connection also on a standard telephone line or a cable connection, using cables wired for television use. The latter two options come under the general term of broadband as they offer much faster connections (and therefore download speeds) than a dial-up connection. In general, broadband connections are up to 10 times faster than dial-up. Whichever connection you use, there are settings that can be applied to ensure your Internet experience works as smoothly as possible.

*One option for connecting to the Internet is by using the Internet Connect program in the Applications folder.*

*Once you have connected to the Internet you still have to open a browser to browse the Web or an email program to send email.*

## Settings for a dial-up modem

1 Open System Preferences and select the Network preference

2 Click here and select the Internal Modem option

*AOL users can use separate settings by selecting AOL Dial-up in the Configure box, instead of PPP.*

3 Click the TCP/IP tab

4 Click here and select Using PPP

5 Click the PPP tab

6 Enter the account details (these will be provided by your Internet Service Provider)

7 Click here for further PPP options

9 Click Apply Now

8 Select the additional options and click OK

*If you check on the "Connect automatically when needed" box you may find that your dial-up connection becomes active automatically. To avoid this, check this box off.*

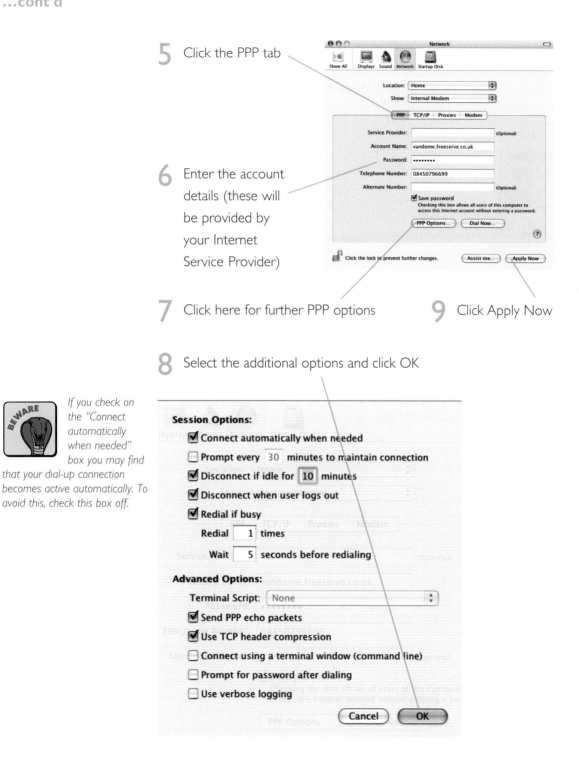

**Session Options:**

☑ **Connect automatically when needed**

☐ Prompt every `30` minutes to maintain connection

☑ **Disconnect if idle for** `10` **minutes**

☑ **Disconnect when user logs out**

☑ **Redial if busy**

Redial `1` times

Wait `5` seconds before redialing

**Advanced Options:**

**Terminal Script:** `None`

☑ **Send PPP echo packets**

☑ **Use TCP header compression**

☐ **Connect using a terminal window (command line)**

☐ **Prompt for password after dialing**

☐ **Use verbose logging**

Cancel     OK

## Connecting via a dial-up modem

Once the settings for a dial-up modem have been applied, the Internet can be accessed in two ways:

*If you are having problems connecting to the Internet, select Open Internet Connect and check the relevant settings.*

Click here on the Apple Menu bar and select Connect

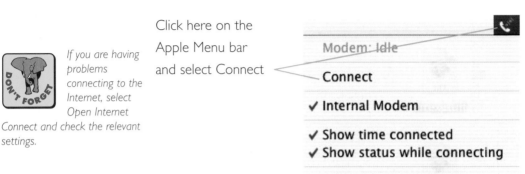

Select Open Internet Connect, above, (or open it from the Applications folder) and select Connect. This can also be used to enter a different configuration for the modem

## Settings for an Ethernet connection

Since a DSL or cable connection via an Ethernet cable is "always on", there is no need to connect to the Internet each time you want to go online, as you do with a dial-up connection. This means that you only need to apply the required settings and you should then be able to access the Internet via your ISP. To apply the settings for an Ethernet connection:

1 Open System Preferences and select the Network preference

*DHCP stands for Dynamic Host Configuration Protocol and is a method for automatically obtaining all of the details that are required to connect to the Internet. Once you click Apply Now, the settings will be obtained and applied. After this, you should be able to use your Internet connection, although you may have to reboot the computer first.*

2 Click here and select the Built-in Ethernet option

3 Click the TCP/IP tab

4 Click here and select Using DHCP

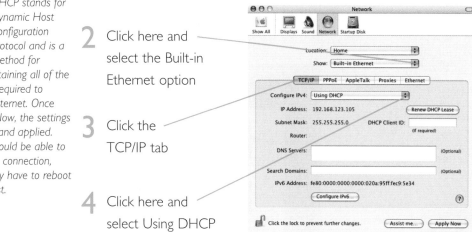

or

*Settings for connecting to the Internet via an Ethernet connection can also be applied manually, in which case you would need to get the necessary information from your ISP. However, in the majority of cases, the Using DHCP option should do the trick.*

If it is a PPoE connection, click here and enter the required settings which should have been provided by your ISP

5 Click Apply Now

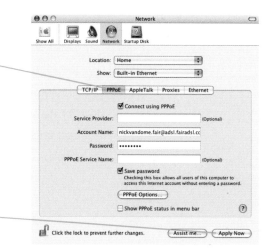

# Safari

Safari is a Web browser that is designed specifically to be used with OS X. It is similar in most respects to other browsers, but it usually functions more quickly and works seamlessly with OS X Panther.

## Safari overview

1. Click here on the Dock to launch Safari

*There is a version of Internet Explorer that can be used with OS X, but as Safari is designed specifically for the operating system it usually works more efficiently than the former.*

Back and forward

Page refresh

Address bar

Google search

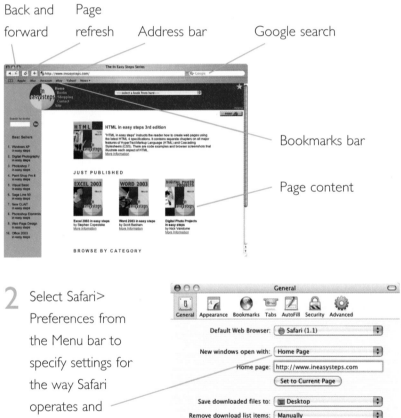

Bookmarks bar

Page content

*If the Address Bar is not visible, select View from the Menu bar and check on the Address Bar option. From this menu you can also select or deselect items such as the Back/Forward buttons, the Stop/Reload buttons and the Google Search box.*

2. Select Safari> Preferences from the Menu bar to specify settings for the way Safari operates and displays Web pages

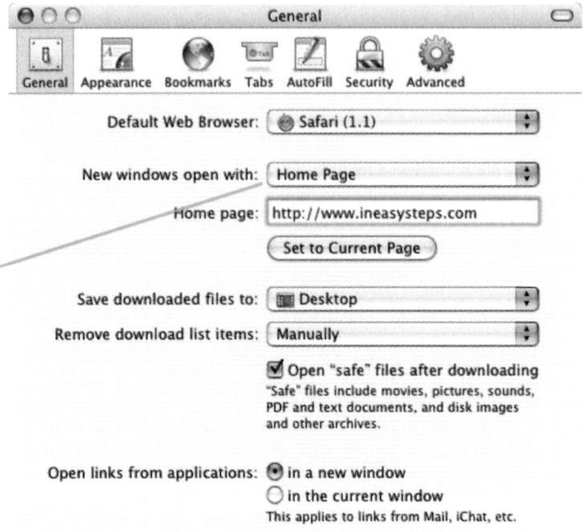

## Adding bookmarks

Bookmarks are a device by which you can create quick links to your favorite Web pages or the ones you visit most frequently. Bookmarks can be added to a menu or the Bookmarks bar in Safari which makes them even quicker to access. Folders can also be created to store the less frequently used bookmarks. To view and create bookmarks:

1 Click here to view all bookmarks

*Only keep your most frequently used bookmarks in the Bookmarks Bar. Otherwise some of them will cease to be visible, as there will be too many entries for the available space.*

2 All of the saved bookmarks are displayed in the Bookmarks window. Click here to add a new folder

*If you are registered for the .Mac service, you can upload all of your bookmarks to your online account and you will be able to access them from any computer with an Internet connection. For more details on this, see Chapter Seven.*

3 Click here to create a bookmark for the page currently being viewed

4 Enter a name for the bookmark and select a location in which to store it

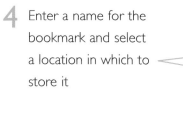

Type a name for the bookmark, and choose where to keep it.

The In Easy Steps Series

Bookmarks Bar

Cancel     Add

5 Click Add

# Mail

The OS X email program, simply called Mail, can be used for all standard email functions and it also has an effective system for identifying, blocking and removing junk email (spam), one of the great blights on the Internet. Before using Mail it can be useful to set a few preferences. To do this, open Mail and select Mail>Preferences from the Menu bar.

Click here to access the General preferences. These can be used to set how often Mail checks for incoming messages and also for choosing an alert sound when new mail arrives

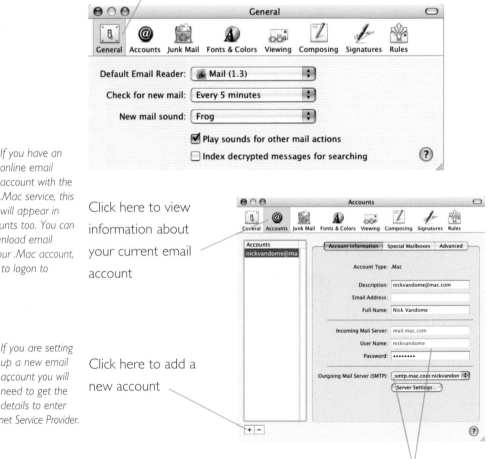

*If you have an online email account with the .Mac service, this will appear in your Mail accounts too. You can use this to download email directly from your .Mac account, without having to logon to .Mac first.*

Click here to view information about your current email account

*If you are setting up a new email account you will need to get the details to enter from your Internet Service Provider.*

Click here to add a new account

Enter details for the new account here

## Receiving and sending emails

Click here to reply to a message

Click here to write a new message

Click here to download new messages

*Mail can download messages from all of the accounts that you have set up within the Accounts preference.*

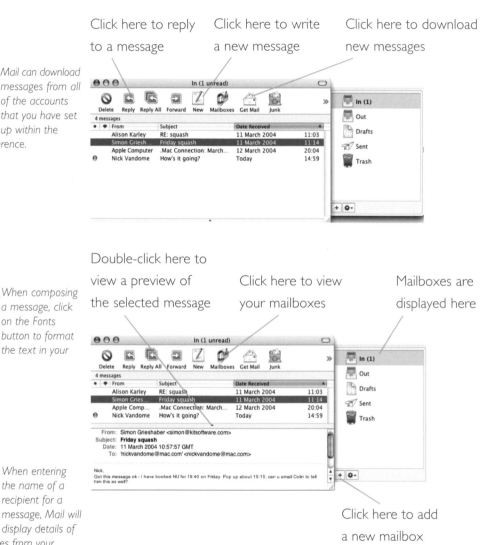

Double-click here to view a preview of the selected message

Click here to view your mailboxes

Mailboxes are displayed here

*When composing a message, click on the Fonts button to format the text in your message.*

*When entering the name of a recipient for a message, Mail will display details of matching names from your Address Book. For instance, if you type DA, all of the entries in your Address Book beginning with this will be displayed and you can select the required one.*

Click here to add a new mailbox

To compose a new message, click on the New button, enter details here and click Send

## Dealing with junk email

Junk email is the scourge of the Internet but it is possible to "train" Mail to identify and remove unwanted messages. To do this:

1 Select Mail>Preferences from the Menu bar and click on the Junk Mail button

2 Check on this box

3 Check on this box. This will enable Mail to build up a pattern for junk mail items

*Once you are content that you have trained Mail to deal with junk mail, check on the "Move it to the junk mailbox (Automatic)" option under the When Junk Mail Arrives heading. This will then automatically remove junk mail when it arrives, although it will still need to be deleted from the Trash folder manually.*

4 In your Inbox, select an item of junk mail and click here. This will help Mail identify different types of junk mail that may have escaped its own filters

# iChat

iChat is the instant messaging service that is provided with OS X. It can be used by members of the .Mac online service or by AOL members who have access to the AOL Instant Messenger (AIM) service. iChat supports instant text messaging, telephone messaging and also video messaging (with the appropriate hardware). To use iChat:

*Preferences for how iChat operates can be chosen by selecting iChat> Preferences from the Menu bar.*

I Click on this icon on the Dock or in the Applications folder

*A Buddy List is a list of contacts you want to chat to via iChat.*

2 Click here to show your online status. If you select Available, this means that other people can contact you for chatting

*You have to be connected to the Internet in order to be able to use iChat.*

3 Click here to select an image for your online profile. This can be a graphic or a photograph of yourself

4 Click here to add a new buddy i.e. someone to chat to

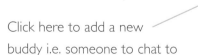

5 Select a contact from your Address Book

If you choose a contact from your Address Book, they must have the details of a .Mac account entered or details of an AIM account.

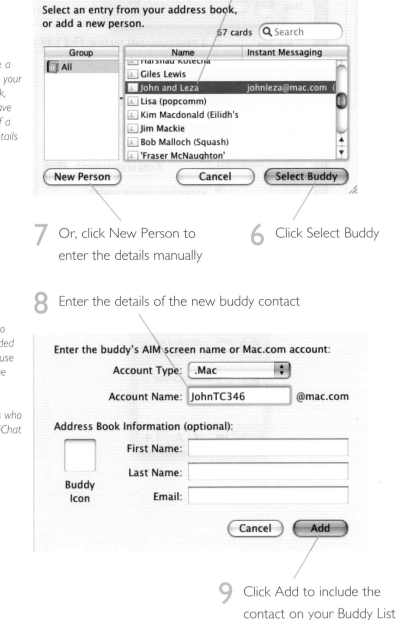

**Select an entry from your address book, or add a new person.**

57 cards 🔍 Search

| Group | Name | Instant Messaging |
|-------|------|-------------------|
| 📁 All | Harshad Kotecha | |
| | Giles Lewis | |
| | John and Leza | johnleza@mac.com |
| | Lisa (popcomm) | |
| | Kim Macdonald (Eilidh's | |
| | Jim Mackie | |
| | Bob Malloch (Squash) | |
| | 'Fraser McNaughton' | |

[ New Person ]          [ Cancel ]          [ Select Buddy ]

7 Or, click New Person to enter the details manually

6 Click Select Buddy

8 Enter the details of the new buddy contact

If you want to find like-minded people who use iChat, visit the website at www.ichatfinder.com. This contains numerous contacts who are willing to participate in iChat conversations.

**Enter the buddy's AIM screen name or Mac.com account:**

Account Type:  [ .Mac ▼ ]

Account Name:  [ JohnTC346 ]  @mac.com

**Address Book Information (optional):**

Buddy Icon

First Name:  [                    ]

Last Name:  [                    ]

Email:  [                    ]

[ Cancel ]    [ Add ]

9 Click Add to include the contact on your Buddy List

## Beginning to chat

Once you have added contacts to your Buddy List, you can start chatting with people. To do this:

1 Click on a contact on your Buddy List

*If a buddy has a green circle next to their name, it means that they are currently online and available for chatting.*

2 Click here to begin a text chat

*The appearance of the text for your iChat conversation can be formatted in the iChat preferences.*

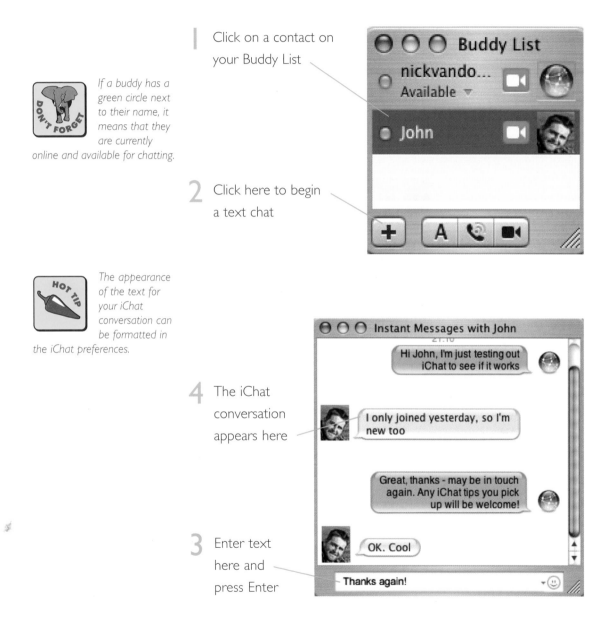

4 The iChat conversation appears here

3 Enter text here and press Enter

# iChat AV

iChat AV operates in the same way as iChat, except that it uses video for communication rather than text. To use iChat AV you require a broadband Internet connection and the iSight video camera, that can be attached to any Mac. To use iChat AV:

*Other types of webcams can be used with iChat AV, but the iSight one works most effectively and provides excellent quality.*

1 Open iChat and select a buddy

2 Click here to view your own video screen

3 Click here to invite the buddy to a video chat

4 Before the video chat starts your image appears here. Once the chat starts this is minimized, but still visible, and the other person's image takes up the main part of the screen

*iChat AV allows for full screen video and audio simultaneously. This means that there is no delay in either, when you are engaged in a video chat.*

5 Click here to select preferences for the way iChat AV operates

*Because of its speed and quality, iChat AV is a genuine option for video conferencing in a business environment.*

6 Preferences can be selected for the type of camera used, the microphone and the type of connection

# Sherlock

Sherlock has been a regular feature of the Apple operating system over the years. Traditionally, it has been used to search for items on a Mac's hard drive but in OS X Panther it has evolved into a facility for searching for items on the World Wide Web. However, unlike most search engines, Sherlock offers different channels of information which can be used to search for specific items such as movies in a particular area, telephone numbers, flights or meanings of words. It is this targeted searching that elevates Sherlock above search engines that operate on general word searches. To use Sherlock:

1    Click on this icon on the Dock or in the Applications folder

2    Click here to access specific channels

3    Click a channel to view its contents

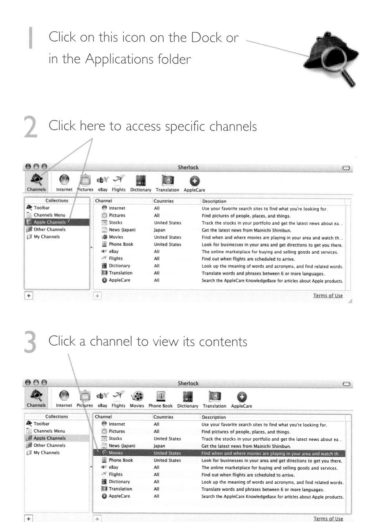

**4** Enter details for the items for which you want to search

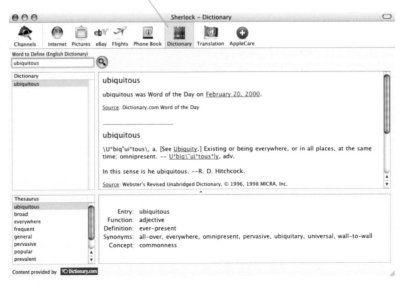

**5** After a few seconds the requested information will be displayed

**6** Click on the toolbar to move to a different channel

*Some channels have search boxes for entering specific words or phrases, such as the Dictionary. Others have drop-down lists from which you can choose the required options.*

# Using .Mac

If you are looking for an online extension for your Mac and OS X, then .Mac is the service for you. It is an online service for Mac users that provides 100 Mb of storage space on the Internet and also a variety of functions ranging from creating Web pages to downloading valuable virus protection. This chapter shows how to join the .Mac world and covers the various options that are then available.

## Covers

**Chapter Seven**

# Registering for .Mac

.Mac is the online service from Apple that enables you to store files on one of the Apple computers on the Web. These files can then be accessed from any computer that is connected to the Internet and they can also be shared with other Web users. In addition to file storing and sharing .Mac also offers a variety of services:

- Online email (Mac Mail)

- Creating and publishing websites (HomePage)

- Sending electronic greeting cards (iCards)

- Publishing calendars and your address book

- File backup (Backup)

- Virus protection (Virex)

.Mac is a subscription service, but before committing yourself to this, it is possible to register for a trial period of 60 days to see how the service works and if you can make use of it. To register for the 60 day trial, go to the website at www.mac.com and click on the Try Now button. You will need to enter some registration information such as a username and a password that can be used to access .Mac once you have registered. To register for the full service:

*Your storage space on .Mac is known as iDisk and you can also copy a version of this to your own hard drive. For more details about this, see pages 130–136.*

Access the .Mac website at www.mac.com and click here to start the registration process

**...cont'd**

2 Enter the login details which you would have been given when using the trial version of .Mac. Click Enter

*If you have not registered for the trial version of .Mac, you will complete the registration process, at which point you will be given a username and a password.*

*Whenever you log on to your .Mac account you will need to enter your password, although your member name should be preinserted.*

3 Enter your registration details

*You must check on the "I accept the Terms and Conditions" box before you can move on to the next step of the registration process.*

Please provide the following information to upgrade your .Mac account. .Mac is available to those who are 13 years of age or older.

Member Name: **nickvandome**

**Personal Information**

First Name
Nick

Last Name
Vandome

Country
United Kingdom

Select your preferred language for communications
English

**Referral Information**

Referral Program (optional)
If you were referred by a .Mac member, please enter his or her full .Mac email address below (ie.steve@mac.com).

**Terms and Conditions**

You need to accept the Terms and Conditions to signup for .Mac.

☑ **I accept the Terms and Conditions.**

**Additional Information**

You're in control. You always have access to your personal information and contact preferences, so you can change them at any time. To learn how Apple safeguards your personal information, please review the Apple Customer Privacy Policy.

☑ Keep me updated with Apple News, special offers, and information about related products and services from other companies.

☑ Keep me updated with .Mac Newsletter and other .Mac-specific communications.

Where will you primarily use .Mac?
Choose...

What is your level of experience with Macs?
Choose...

I Have An Activation Key

Continue

4 Click Continue to move through the registration process

# iDisk

iDisk is your own personal storage space within the .Mac service. It can be used to store files for sharing, backing up your hard drive files or storing files for use in other parts of .Mac. Once you have registered for .Mac, your iDisk will be activated. Once this has been done, you can access it by selecting Go>iDisk>My iDisk from the Finder Menu bar. As long as you are connected to the Internet, the iDisk icon will be displayed in the Finder and also on your Desktop. When you disconnect from the Internet, the icon will disappear from the Desktop, but it will remain in the Finder. By default, items can only be added to the iDisk when you are connected to the Internet.

*You can view more information about your iDisk, such as how much storage space you have used up, and apply various settings within the .Mac preferences in System Preferences.*

1 The iDisk icon is displayed as a separate volume in the Finder

2 There are separate folders within iDisk and they are displayed here

# Adding files to iDisk

Within iDisk there are nine folders. Three of these, Backup, Library and Software, are read-only folders for use with the .Mac service. The Public folder is for sharing files over the Internet. The remaining folders can all have files added to them from your hard drive. To do this:

*The folders which can be used to store your own files are Documents, Pictures, Movies, Sites and Music. The Pictures folder is used by .Mac for items requiring images (such as iCards) and the Sites folder is used for Web pages by the HomePage function on .Mac.*

1 Select files in the Finder and drag them over the iDisk icon and hold the mouse until the iDisk opens

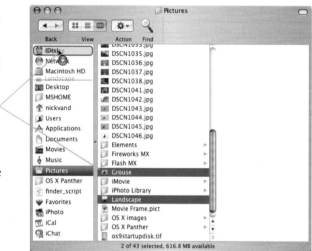

2 Hold the files over the required folder until it opens. Drop the files into the open folder

*Documents can also be saved directly to the iDisk from any application by using the Save As command and then selecting the required folder within iDisk as the destination.*

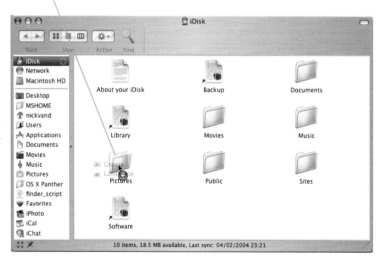

# Creating a local copy of iDisk

By default, you have to be connected to the Internet in order to access your iDisk and add files to it. However, it is also possible to create a copy of the iDisk on your own hard drive. This is known as a local copy and it enables you to add files to your iDisk even when you are not connected to the Internet. Then, when you do connect, the local version can automatically be synchronized with the remote copy so that they both contain the same items. To do this:

1 Access System Preferences from the Dock and select the .Mac preference. Check this box on and select the Automatically option

*If you are unsure about synchronizing your iDisk, check on the Manually box for the synchronize option. When you have synchronized using this method you can then apply the Automatically setting.*

2 The presence of a local version of iDisk is denoted by this icon

*If you have a dial-up connection to the Internet it could take a long time to upload certain items to your online iDisk, particularly for large documents or high resolution image files.*

3 When a connection is made to the Internet the local and remote versions of iDisk are synchronized i.e. any items that have been added to the local version are copied to the remote version

# Sharing with iDisk

As soon as you connect to the Internet you have access to the contents of your remote iDisk (if you have created a local copy then you will have access to this regardless of whether you are connected to the Internet or not). In addition, you can also access the contents of the personal folders within your iDisk from any computer (Mac or PC) that has an Internet connection. To do this, visit the .Mac website at www.mac.com and enter your .Mac login details. You will then have access to the .Mac services and you will be able to use the files on your iDisk as required.

As well as using your own iDisk files on the Web, it is also possible to let other people share them. This means that you can distribute a variety of files such as pictures, movies and large documents without having to email them to people. The process of sharing iDisk files consists of two main steps:

- Adding files to the Public folder within iDisk

- Ensuring that the intended recipient has the required utility to enable them to view the Public folder on your iDisk

To do this:

Add files to the Public folder of your iDisk. If necessary, synchronize your local and remote versions to ensure that the new files are available over the Internet

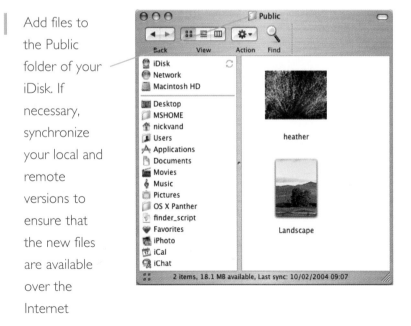

2 For the person who is going to share the files, go to the .Mac website at www.mac.com and click on the iDisk icon

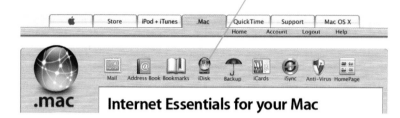

*If you are downloading the iDisk utility you do not have to login to the .Mac service, so anyone can do it, not just .Mac members.*

3 Click on the link for accessing the relevant utility (there is one for use on a Mac and also a Windows version – the example here is for the Windows version)

*The iDisk utility is very small and only takes a couple of minutes to download, even if you are using a dial-up modem connection.*

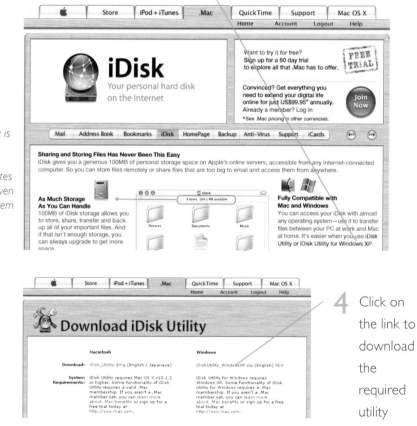

4 Click on the link to download the required utility

5 Click Save to download the utility to your hard drive. For ease of use, this can be the desktop. Then double-click on the utility's icon to install it

*For Windows, the default location for the utility once it has been installed is Program Files>.Mac Utilities> iDisk Utility for Windows.*

6 Open the folder in which the utility is located and double-click on its icon to open the program

*If you want to access your own iDisk from another computer, check on the iDisk box and enter your .Mac password. If someone else is accessing your iDisk they will only be able to access the Public Folder within your iDisk. For this they will require your .Mac member name but not a password.*

7 Check on the Public Folder button, enter the member name of the .Mac account and click Connect

8 A confirmation box states that the Public Folder has been mounted. This means it is available to view from your computer. Click OK

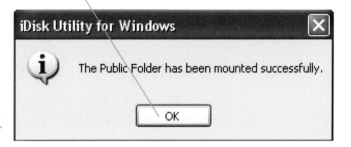

*When items are viewed on your iDisk they can be copied onto other user's computers with the Copy and Paste commands.*

9 The Public folder is displayed as a Network Drive in Windows Explorer. Double-click to view its contents

*For Mac users, the relevant Disk Utility is downloaded and installed into the Utilities folder.*

# Mail

For each .Mac service, you have to login at the .Mac homepage (www.mac.com) and then select the required option. Once you have logged in, you do not have to do so again for subsequent service.

.Mac Mail is an online email service that allows you to send and receive emails from any computer that is connected to the Internet. It can be used as a home email service and it is also an excellent way to keep in touch when away from home such as on a business trip or on holiday. To use .Mac Mail:

Click here to download messages

Click here to create new messages

Click here to access different mail boxes

If you have a .Mac mail account this will also be available via the OS X email program, Mail. In some cases it will be your default email account.

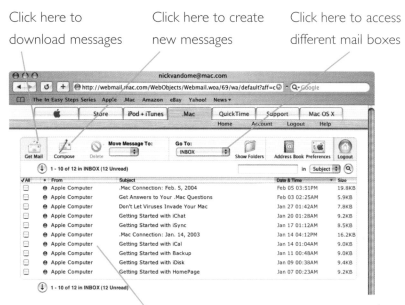

Messages are displayed here. Double-click on one to view its contents

To compose a new email, enter the details and click Send

If you have synchronized your OS X Address Book with your .Mac one, all of your contacts will be available when entering recipients for your email messages.

# Address Book

The .Mac Address Book is an online version of the OS X Panther Address Book. By using the synchronization features within OS X Panther it is possible to make sure that the online and offline versions of the Address Book are the same. This means that you can always access up to date information from your Address Book wherever you are. To use the .Mac Address Book:

Click here to view the contents of the Address Book

Click here to add a new contact

 The online and offline versions of your Address Book can be synchronized with the iSync program (see Chapter Five for full details). This works both ways i.e. if you update the .Mac Address Book, iSync will update the version on your hard drive, and vice versa.

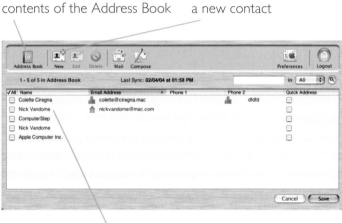

Double-click on an entry to view its details

 Address Book details can also be added to external devices such as handheld computers, cell phones and even the iPod. iSync works with these devices too.

Click here to edit the details of the selected contact

Click here to delete the current contact

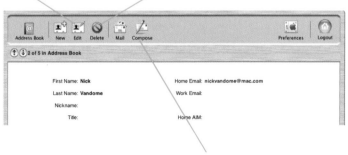

Click here to send an email to the current contact

# Bookmarks

.Mac Bookmarks can be used to transfer the bookmarks that you have added to the Safari Web browser. This enables you to have access to your bookmarks from any Internet enabled computer, rather than having to recreate them if you are working away from your own computer. To use .Mac Bookmarks:

1 To copy existing bookmarks, click the Sync Now button

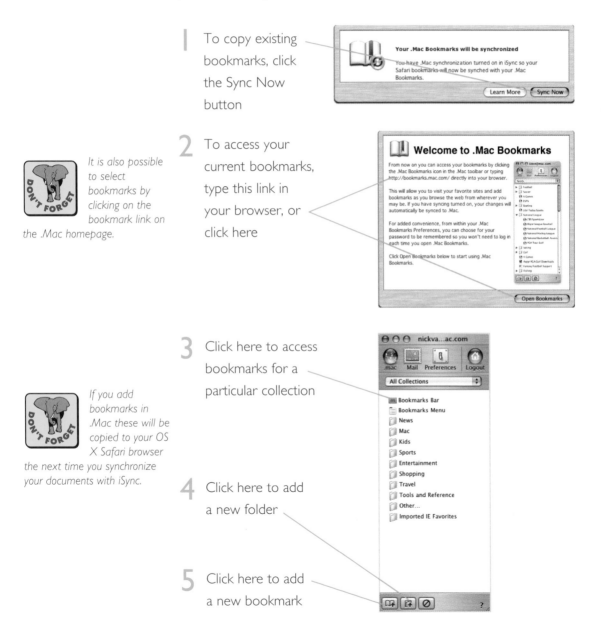

*It is also possible to select bookmarks by clicking on the bookmark link on the .Mac homepage.*

2 To access your current bookmarks, type this link in your browser, or click here

3 Click here to access bookmarks for a particular collection

*If you add bookmarks in .Mac these will be copied to your OS X Safari browser the next time you synchronize your documents with iSync.*

4 Click here to add a new folder

5 Click here to add a new bookmark

# HomePage

.Mac HomePage is the online Web publishing program that enables you to create and publish your own Web pages, without having to know any of the technicalities of Web page creation. HomePage can create pages with pre-designed templates and themes. To create Web pages with HomePage:

*The Themes within HomePage are more varied and diverse than on some other online Web publishing sites.*

Click here to select a theme for your Web page

*The Photo Album theme uses images in your iDisk Pictures folders to create an online display of your photos.*

2 Select images to add to your Web page

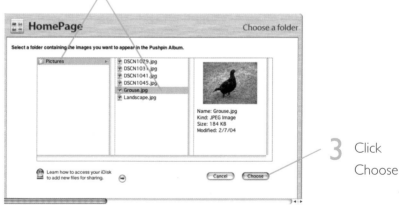

3 Click Choose

4 Click here to add text to the Web page

If there are several spaces for text boxes on a page, make sure that they are all completed before the page is published, otherwise there may be gaps on the completed page.

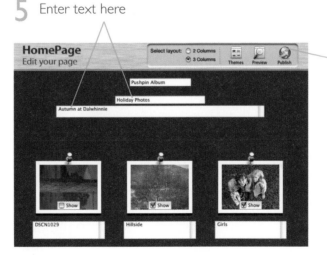

5 Enter text here

It is possible to create additional pages for a HomePage website and also add extra sites within individual Web addresses.

6 Click here to publish the Web page

Try and view your published page on different computers and different Web browsers. This will give you an idea of any inconsistencies between systems.

7 Click here to view the Web page

# iCards

iCards is a .Mac service that can be used to send electronic greetings cards. They can be created using preset iCards templates or you can use your own images to create personalized cards. To use iCards:

*If you are sending an iCard, make sure the recipient accesses their computer and their email regularly, otherwise it could be a waste of time.*

**1** Click here to select a preset design for your card

or

Click here to select your own images for your card

**2** Click here to view an image from the Pictures folder of your iDisk

*Click on the Preview button to view a thumbnail of the selected image.*

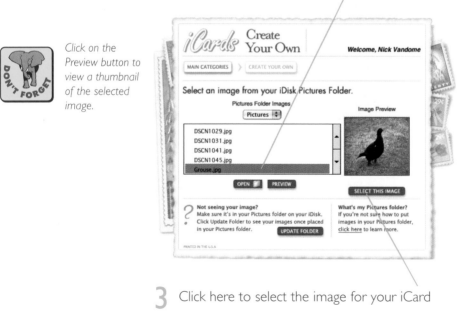

**3** Click here to select the image for your iCard

4 Enter text here

5 Select a font here

6 Click Continue

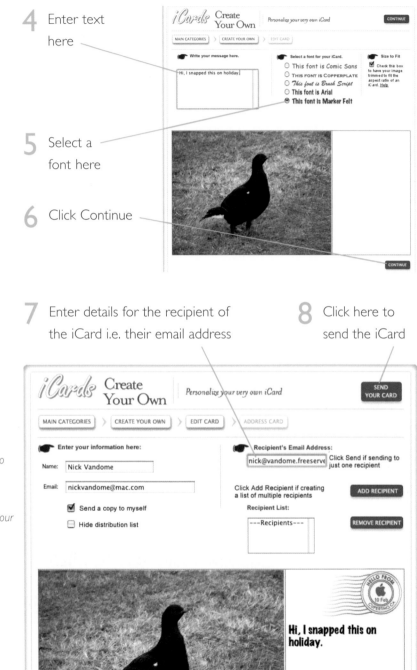

7 Enter details for the recipient of the iCard i.e. their email address

8 Click here to send the iCard

*Check on the "Send a copy to myself" box to verify that the card has been sent and to keep a copy for your records, if required.*

# Backup

Backup is a program that can be downloaded from .Mac and used to backup your data to a variety of locations. This can be any folder on your hard drive, an external device (such as an external hard drive or even an iPod) or your iDisk on the .Mac server. To download Backup:

*Backup is only available with a full .Mac membership, rather than the trial version.*

| Click here on the .Mac homepage

2 Click here and follow the downloading instructions

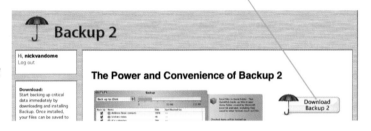

*If you are backing up to iDisk, the maximum amount of data that you can include is 100 Mb. If the selected items exceed this limit a red bar will appear at the top of the Backup window.*

## Using Backup

| Open Backup from the Applications folder

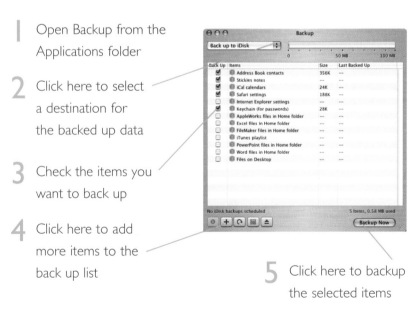

2 Click here to select a destination for the backed up data

3 Check the items you want to back up

4 Click here to add more items to the back up list

5 Click here to backup the selected items

# Virex

Virex is a powerful anti-virus program that can be downloaded from .Mac and used to protect your data. To do this:

I Click here on the .Mac homepage

 *Virex is only available with a full .Mac membership, rather than the trial version.*

2 Click here and follow the downloading instructions

 *When you first run Virex, you may be asked to update the program's virus definitions. This is to ensure that it is as up to date as possible. These are known as eUpdates and the program will be updated frequently in this way.*

## Using Virex

I Open Virex from the Applications folder

2 Click here to select a volume or a folder over which you want to scan

 *Click on the Virus Info button to get up to date information about the latest viruses.*

3 Click here to scan over the selected item

4 Results are shown here

# iCal

Although iCal can work perfectly well as an offline calendar, it is also possible to use it in conjunction with .Mac to create online versions. This enables you to view them from any computer and also allow other people to view them online. To do this:

1 Open the offline version of iCal and select Calendar>Publish from the Menu bar

2 Select the options for the calendar and click Publish

*Options for synchronizing your offline calendars with any that have been published on .Mac can be found in the iSync program. For more information on this, see Chapter Five.*

**Publish name:**

Home

☐ Publish changes automatically
☑ Publish subjects and notes
☐ Publish alarms
☐ Publish To Do items

**Publish calendar** [ on .Mac ▼ ]

**Status:** ▨▨▨▨▨▨▨▨▨

( Cancel )  ( Publish )

3 Once the calendar is published on .Mac you will be sent a Web address at which the calendar can be viewed. Click Visit Page to view the calendar or click Send Mail to send the Web address to people who you want to have online access to the calendar

○ ○ ○            **Calendar Published**

**Your Calendar 'Home' has been published successfully, and can be subscribed at URL:**

webcal://ical.mac.com/nickvandome/Home.ics

**or be viewed with a browser at URL:**

http://ical.mac.com/nickvandome/Home

( Visit Page )      ( Send Mail )    ( OK )

# Multiple users

This chapter looks at how OS X can be used to allow multiple users access to their own individual working environment on the same computer. It shows how to set up different user accounts and how to customize your workspace.

## Covers

Chapter Eight

# About user accounts

OS X enables multiple users to access individual accounts on the same computer. If there are multiple users, i.e. two or more, for a single machine, each person can sign on individually and access their own files and folders. In addition, they can also access their own system settings and customize their workspace in exactly the way they want. This means that each person can have their own individual style for the desktop, the Dock and the Finder. When they log out and someone else logs in, the new user's preferences will be available, in exactly the same way as they left them the last time they used the computer. This form of access is known as user accounts and OS X remembers the settings and preferences for each individual user. To access and create user accounts:

*Every computer with multiple users has at least one main user, also known as an administrator. This means that they have greater control over the number of items that they can edit and alter. If there is only one user on a computer, they automatically take on the role of the administrator. Administrators have a particularly important role to play when computers are networked together. Each computer can potentially have several administrators.*

Open the System Preferences and click on the Accounts preference

# Adding users

Once the Accounts preference has been accessed it is possible to add, delete and edit details about users. To add a new user:

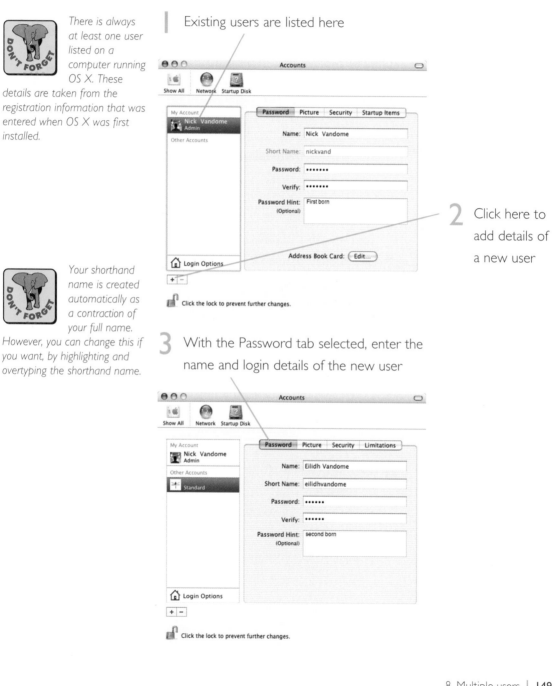

*There is always at least one user listed on a computer running OS X. These details are taken from the registration information that was entered when OS X was first installed.*

*Your shorthand name is created automatically as a contraction of your full name. However, you can change this if you want, by highlighting and overtyping the shorthand name.*

**1** Existing users are listed here

**2** Click here to add details of a new user

**3** With the Password tab selected, enter the name and login details of the new user

## ...cont'd

*If an administrator forgets their password, insert the OS X CD while holding down the C key. Once this opens, select Installer>Reset Password from the Menu bar. Then select the correct user and enter a new password. Click on Save to apply the changes.*

**4** Click the Picture tab and select an image for the new user. Click Edit to browse your hard drive to use one of your own images

*Unless you have particular security concerns, it is probably best not to set a Master Password for your computer.*

**5** If required, click the Security tab and click Set Master Password to create a security password for the computer, rather than the new user

**6** Click the Limitations tab to assign any limits on the new user for what they can and cannot change on the computer

# Deleting users

Once a user has been added their name appears on the list in the Accounts preference dialog box. It is then possible to edit the details of a particular user or delete them altogether. To do this:

1 Select a user from the list

*Always tell other users if you are planning to delete them from the system. Don't just remove them and then let them find out the next time they try to login. If you delete a user, their personal files are left untouched and can still be accessed.*

2 Click here to remove the selected person's user account

3 A warning box appears to check if you really do want to delete the selected user. If you do, click on Delete Immediately

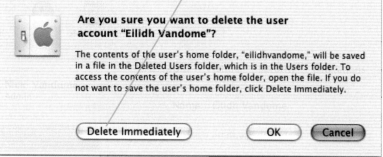

# Logging out

If you have your computer set up for multiple users, i.e. you have several user accounts, each user can access their own account in two ways. They can logon as themselves when the computer is first turned on, or one user can log out while OS X is running and then another user can log in. To do this:

*If you log out it does not shut down the computer. It just brings up the login window so that other users can login if they want to.*

1 Select Apple menu> Log Out from the Menu bar

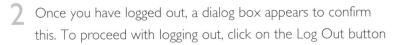

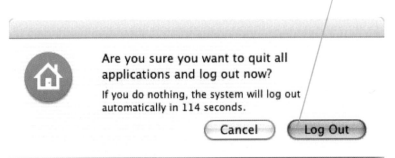

2 Once you have logged out, a dialog box appears to confirm this. To proceed with logging out, click on the Log Out button

**Are you sure you want to quit all applications and log out now?**

If you do nothing, the system will log out automatically in 114 seconds.

Cancel    Log Out

# Fast user switching

If you do not want to go through the process of logging in and out every time that a new user accesses the computer there is also a function for fast user switching. The only drawback of this is that it is not as secure as each user logging out each time someone else wants to use the computer. However, in the majority of cases, this will not be a great issue. To use fast user switching:

1 Open the Accounts preference window under System Preferences

*Click on the Login Options link to specify what happens when the computer is turned on. This can be a list of all of the users on the computer, or it can be set so that the computer automatically opens with the administrator's account, without the need for them to login each time.*

2 Click the Login Options

3 Check on the "Enable fast user switching" box

4 A warning box appears. Click OK to continue

**Warning**

This feature will allow other users to stay logged in and continue running software in the background while you're using this computer. This feature should only be enabled if you trust the other users of this computer.

Cancel    OK

5 The current
user is
displayed at
the top right
of the Mac
menu bar.
Click here to
display other
available users

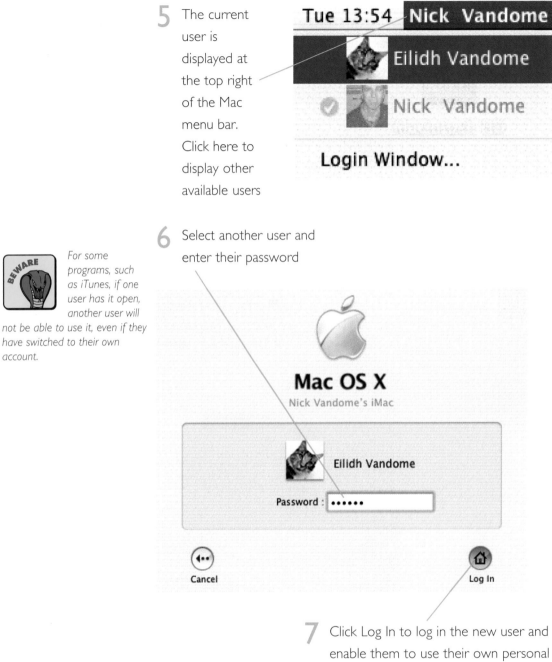

6 Select another user and
enter their password

For some
programs, such
as iTunes, if one
user has it open,
another user will
not be able to use it, even if they
have switched to their own
account.

7 Click Log In to log in the new user and
enable them to use their own personal
settings on the computer

# Customizing your workspace

With multiple user accounts each user can customize the settings and preferences for their own account. These are available each time a user accesses their account, regardless of how many other people have used the computer in between.

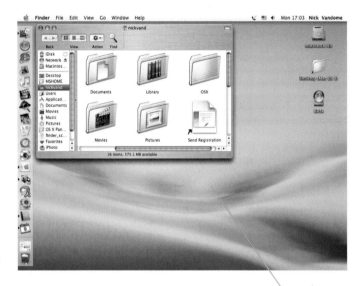

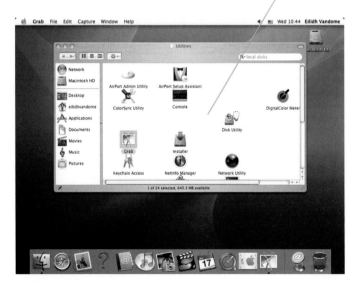

Each user can customize the settings and preferences for their own account. This is always uniquely available to them and no-one else

*Your own workspace will open up exactly as you left it when you last logged out.*

# Viewing user accounts

It is possible for individual users to see the overview of another user's account. They can also exchange files with other users by placing them in a folder called a Drop Box. This means that the user can then access these files the next time they log in to their own account. (Under normal circumstances they would not be able to view any folders or files in someone else's account). To view another user's folders and share files in the Finder:

Select Macintosh HD>Users

*The Users folder also contains the folders of any users that have been deleted. This is where their documents are stored. A system administrator would be able to access these documents and return them to their owner, if required.*

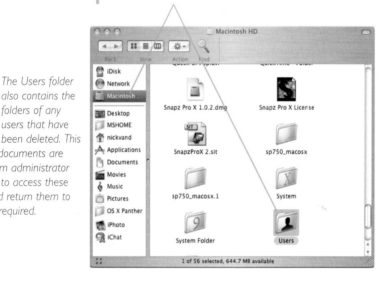

2 Double-click on another user's folder to view its contents

3 Folders
with a No
Entry icon
indicate
that they
cannot be
accessed

*Double-click the Public folder in another user's folder. This contains the Drop Box, into which you can put files for sharing.*

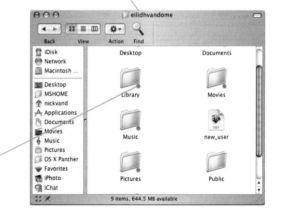

# Advanced features

For users that want to delve a bit more deeply into OS X there are some elements that will keep the most inquisitive computer enthusiast happy. This chapter looks at a few of these elements such as the programming language AppleScript and also how to create a network, share files and share an Internet connection.

## Covers

Chapter Nine

# AppleScript

AppleScript is a programming language which can be used to write your own programs to run on a Mac computer. These can be complex applications or they could be simple utility programs. In addition to writing your own AppleScript, OS X also comes bundled with various scripts that have already been created. These can then be used on your Mac computer. To access the AppleScript options:

*Even for non-programmers, AppleScript is a viable option for creating simple programs that can be used within OS X.*

In the Applications folder, double-click on the AppleScript folder

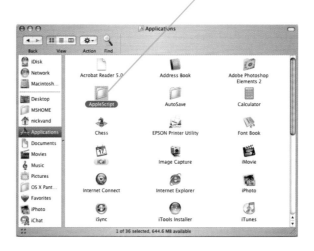

*A good way to gain a general understanding of AppleScript is to look at some of the scripts in the Example Scripts folder and then opening them in Script Editor (double-click on the script name in the Example Scripts folder to open it in Script Editor). This will enable you to see how the scripts are created and the syntax they use.*

The available AppleScript options are available in the folder

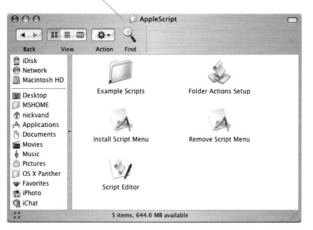

## Launching scripts

To launch existing AppleScripts:

1 Double-click on the Example Scripts folder

*Some AppleScripts are more useful than others. Experiment with different ones to see which best fit your own needs.*

2 Double-click on a script folder

3 Double-click on a script to open it

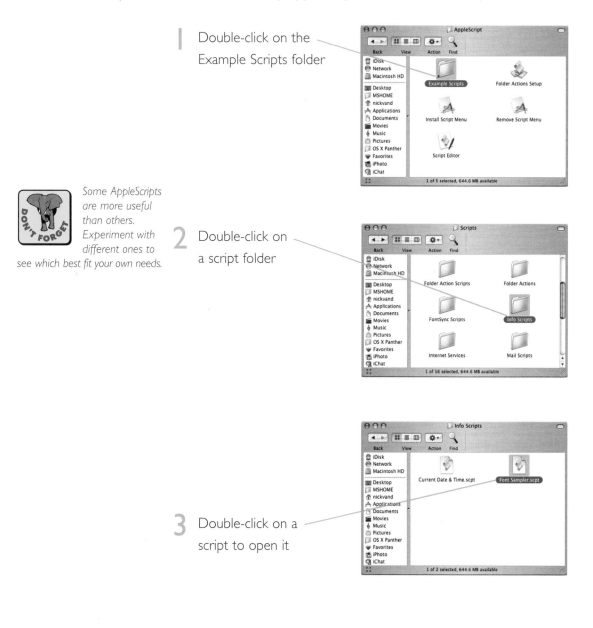

4 The script is
displayed in the
Script Editor

5 Click Run to
execute the script.
An information box
describes the
action of the script.
Click Continue

**Font Sampler**

**This script will use the TextEdit application to create a document containing a sample of each installed typeface.**

Cancel    Continue

6 Once the script is
run, the results are
displayed in the
relevant application,
according to the
type of script

# Writing scripts

If you have some programming knowledge you may want to create your own AppleScripts. To do this:

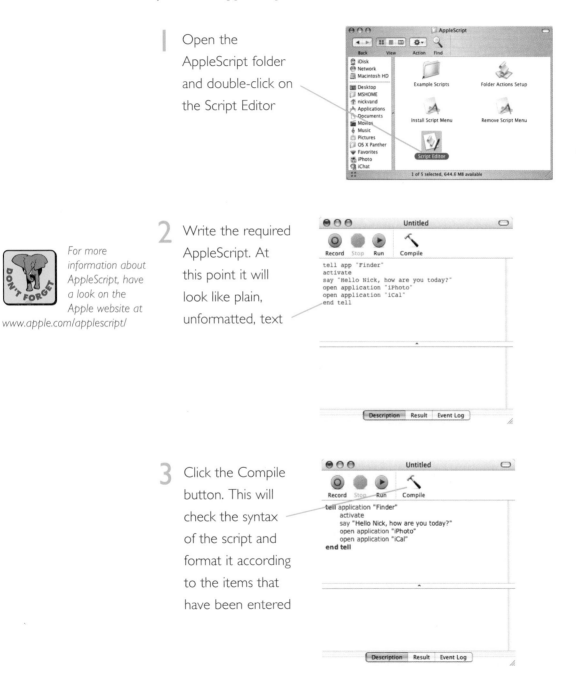

1 Open the AppleScript folder and double-click on the Script Editor

For more information about AppleScript, have a look on the Apple website at www.apple.com/applescript/

2 Write the required AppleScript. At this point it will look like plain, unformatted, text

```
tell app "Finder"
activate
say "Hello Nick, how are you today?"
open application "iPhoto"
open application "iCal"
end tell
```

3 Click the Compile button. This will check the syntax of the script and format it according to the items that have been entered

```
tell application "Finder"
    activate
    say "Hello Nick, how are you today?"
    open application "iPhoto"
    open application "iCal"
end tell
```

4 If there is a problem with the script, the Compiler will display an error message. Click OK to return to the script and correct the syntax error

**Syntax Error**

Expected end of line, etc. but found unknown token.

OK

5 Select File>Save from the Menu bar. Select either Script or Application as the file format

Save As: say_hello
Where: Desktop

File Format: Application
Line Endings: Unix (LF)
Options: ☐ Run Only  ☐ Startup Screen
☐ Stay Open

Cancel   Save

6 Click Save

7 Scripts are denoted by this icon

hello

8 Applications are denoted by this icon

say_hello

# Recording scripts

In addition to writing your own scripts, it is also possible to create them by performing a series of actions, which can be recorded within the Script Editor. This only works with applications that are compatible with AppleScript programming and the Finder is the best starting point for recording scripts. To do this:

1 Open the Script Editor and click the Record button. At this point the document in the Script Editor is empty

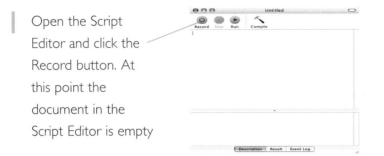

*If you are writing a script for a specific application, such as the Finder, you can check to see commands you can use in AppleScript to control the application. To do this, select File>Open Dictionary from within the Script Editor and double-click the application for which you want to write the script. This will list the commonly used AppleScript terms and commands that can be used.*

2 Access the Finder

3 Perform the required operation (in this example the view option will be set to List and the Finder window resized)

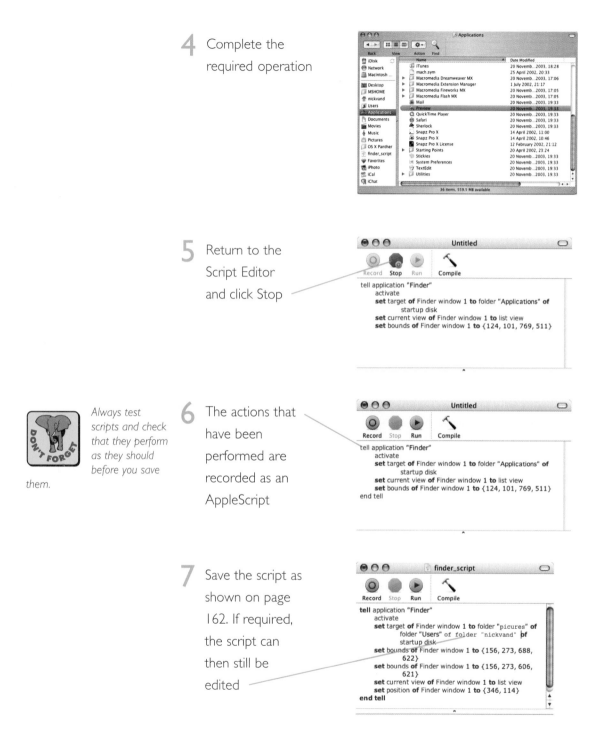

4 Complete the required operation

5 Return to the Script Editor and click Stop

*Always test scripts and check that they perform as they should before you save them.*

6 The actions that have been performed are recorded as an AppleScript

7 Save the script as shown on page 162. If required, the script can then still be edited

# Using scripts

Once scripts have been created and saved they can either be run manually or automatically.

## Using scripts manually

Save the script as an application and double-click on it in its folder or add it to the Finder Sidebar and single click on it here

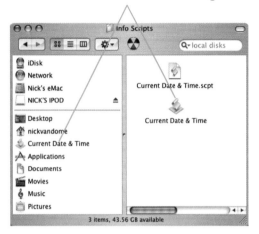

## Using scripts automatically

| Open System Preferences and select the Accounts preference. Click on the Startup Items tab and click here

2 Browse to the required script and click Add to include it in the startup process. The script will then run when the computer is booted up

# Networking overview

Before you start sharing files directly between computers, you have to connect them together. This is known as networking and can be done with two computers in the same room, or with thousands of computers in a major corporation. If you are setting up your own small network it will be known in the computing world as a Local Area Network (LAN). When setting up a network there are various pieces of hardware that are initially required to join all of the required items together. Once this has been done, software settings can be applied for the networked items. Some of the items of hardware that may be required include:

If you have two Macs to be networked and they are in close proximity then this can be achieved with an Ethernet crossover cable. If you have more than two computers, then this is where an Ethernet hub is required. In both cases, there is no need to connect to the Internet to achieve the network.

- A network card. This is known as a Network Interface Card (NIC) and all recent Macs have them built-in

- An Ethernet port and Ethernet cable. This enables you to make the physical connection between devices. Ethernet cables come in a variety of forms but the one you should be looking for is the Cat5E type as this allows for the fastest transfer of data. If you are creating a wireless network then you will not require these

- A hub. This is a piece of hardware with multiple Ethernet ports that enables you to connect all of your devices together and let them communicate with each other. However, conflicts can occur with hubs if two devices try and send data through it at the same time

- A switch. This is similar in operation to a hub but it is more sophisticated in its method of data transfer, thus allowing all of the machines on the network to communicate simultaneously, unlike a hub

Once you have worked out all of the devices that you want to include on your network you can arrange them accordingly. Try and keep the switches and hub within relative proximity of a power supply and, if you are using cables, make sure they are laid out safely.

It is perfectly possible to create a simple network of two computers by joining them with an Ethernet cable and applying the software settings shown on page 168.

## Ethernet network

The cheapest and easiest way to network computers is to create an Ethernet network. This involves buying an Ethernet hub or switch, which enables you to connect several devices to a central point, i.e. the hub or switch. All Apple computers and most modern printers have an Ethernet connection, so it is possible to connect various devices, not just computers. Once all of the devices have been connected by Ethernet cables, you can start applying network settings (see page 168).

## Airport Network

The other option for creating a network is an AirPort network. This is a wireless network and there are two main standards used by Apple computers: Airport, using the IEEE 802.11b standard, which is more commonly known as Wi-Fi, which stands for Wireless Fidelity and the newer Airport Extreme, using the newer IEEE 802.11g standard which is up to 5 times faster than the older 802.11b standard. Thankfully Airport Extreme is also compatible with devices based on the older standard, so one machine loaded with Airport Extreme can still communicate wirelessly with an older Airport one.

*Another method for connecting items wirelessly is called Bluetooth. This covers much shorter distances than Airport and is usually used for items such as printers and cell phones. Bluetooth devices can be connected by using the Bluetooth Setup Assistant in the Utilities folder.*

One of the issues with a wireless network is security since it is possible for someone with a wireless-enabled machine to access your wireless network, if they are within range. However, in the majority of cases the chances of this happening are fairly slim, although it is something you should be aware of.

The basics of a wireless network with Macs is an AirPort card (either Airport or Airport Extreme) installed in all of the required machines and an AirPort base station that can be located anywhere within 150 metres of the AirPort enabled computers. Once the hardware is in place, wireless-enabled devices can be configured by using the Airport Setup Assistant utility found in the Utilities folder. After Airport has been set up the wireless network can be connected. To do this, open the Internet Connect application and select Airport from the toolbar. Then select an available network and click Connect. All of the wireless-enabled devices should then be able to communicate with each other, without the use of a multitude of cables.

# Network settings

Once you have connected the hardware required for a network, you can start applying the network settings that are required for different computers to communicate with one another. To do this (the following example is for networking two Mac computers):

1 In System Preferences, double-click on the Network icon

**Network**

*TCP/IP stands for Transmission Control Protocol/ Internet Protocol. It is a protocol that enables computers on a network, or the Internet, communicate and understand one another.*

2 Click here and select the Built-in Ethernet option

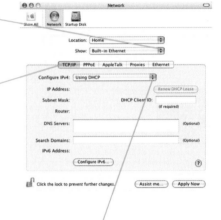

3 Click on the TCP/IP tab (this contains settings that help determine how computers communicate with each other)

4 Click here and select Manually

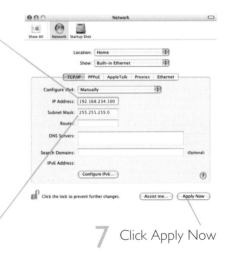

5 Enter the computer's IP address here. This is a series of four sets of three numbers. Use 192 and 168 for the first two sets and numbers between 0 and 255 for the second two sets

*Each computer that you want to include on a network has to have its own unique IP address.*

6 Enter 255.255.255.0 for the Subnet Mask

7 Click Apply Now

# Connecting to a network

Once network settings have been applied to all of the computers that are going to use the network, you can connect them together and create a network. To do this:

You can also connect to another Mac over the Internet by obtaining their public IP address and entering this in the Connect to Server dialog box. To find out a computer's public IP address, select the Sharing preference and click on Personal File Sharing. The IP address should be at the bottom of this window.

1 In Finder, select Go>Connect to Server from the Menu bar

2 Enter the IP address of the computer to which you want to connect

### Connect To Server

**Server Address:**

`192.168.234.100`    **+**    ⊙.

**Favorite Servers:**

🌐 192.168.234.100

( Remove )                ( Browse )  ( **Connect** )

When connecting to a local network, the IP address that is used is known as a private IP address. This means that it is not being used over the Internet. Computers on different networks can use the same private IP addresses as long as they are not going to come in conflict with one another.

3 Click Connect

4 Select an option for how you want to connect to the networked computer and enter any required details

IP addresses for connecting to the Internet are known as public IP addresses and they are unique to ensure that no two devices are trying to use the same address.

Connect to the file server "Nick Vandome's eMac" as:

○ Guest
● Registered User

Name:       Nick Vandome
Password:   ••••••••

( Options... )  ( Cancel )  ( **Connect** )

5 Click Connect

*If you connect to another computer as a guest, you will only be able to access certain parts of the system.*

**6** Select the part of the networked computer to which you want access

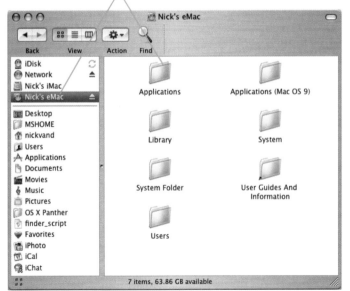

**7** Click OK

*If your network connection does not show up as expected, check that you have enabled Personal File Sharing. See next page for details.*

**8** The networked computer shows up as a new volume in the Finder. If you are the administrator of both machines, you can access the files on the networked machine in the same way as if you were operating that machine

*You can disconnect from a networked computer by ejecting it in the Finder in the same way as you would for a removable drive such as a Zip or CD.*

# File sharing

The main reason for creating a network is being able to share files between different computers. Once the network is up and running there are various options for doing this:

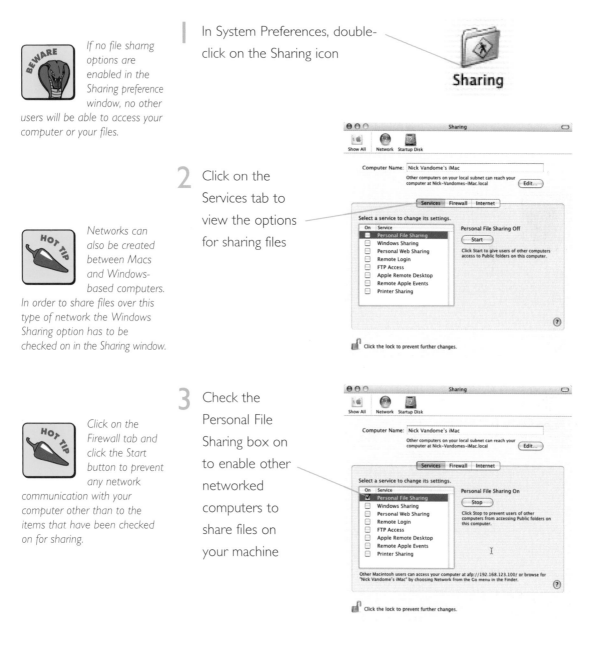

*If no file sharing options are enabled in the Sharing preference window, no other users will be able to access your computer or your files.*

1  In System Preferences, double-click on the Sharing icon

*Networks can also be created between Macs and Windows-based computers. In order to share files over this type of network the Windows Sharing option has to be checked on in the Sharing window.*

2  Click on the Services tab to view the options for sharing files

*Click on the Firewall tab and click the Start button to prevent any network communication with your computer other than to the items that have been checked on for sharing.*

3  Check the Personal File Sharing box on to enable other networked computers to share files on your machine

## Sharing with public folders

If you want to share some of your files with another user rather than give them access to the whole of your computer, this can be done by placing items into a public folder. This can then be accessed by other users (guests) that are networked to your computer. To do this:

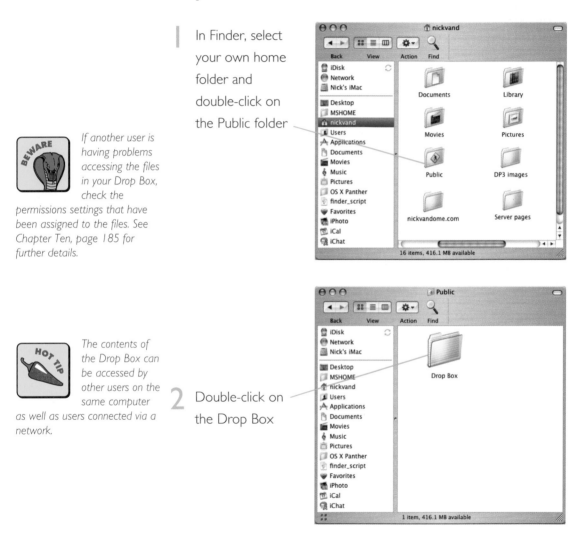

1 In Finder, select your own home folder and double-click on the Public folder

*If another user is having problems accessing the files in your Drop Box, check the permissions settings that have been assigned to the files. See Chapter Ten, page 185 for further details.*

*The contents of the Drop Box can be accessed by other users on the same computer as well as users connected via a network.*

2 Double-click on the Drop Box

3 Place the files you want to share in the Drop Box

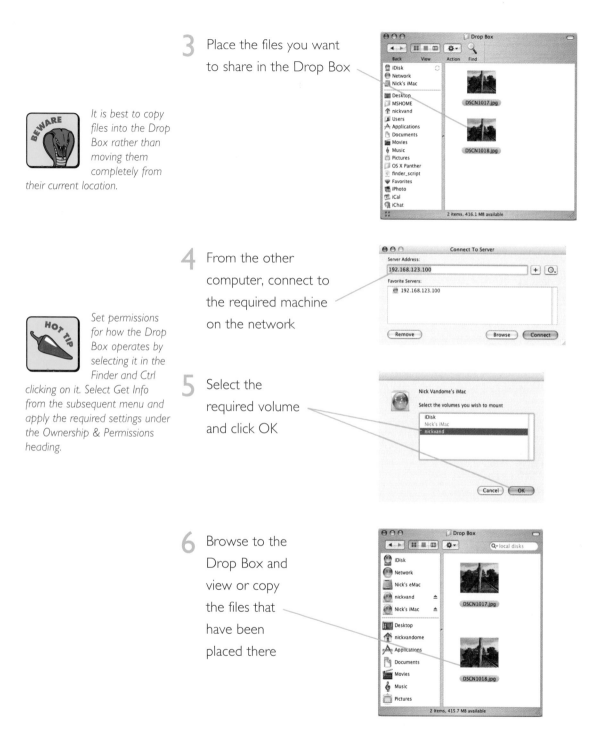

It is best to copy files into the Drop Box rather than moving them completely from their current location.

4 From the other computer, connect to the required machine on the network

Set permissions for how the Drop Box operates by selecting it in the Finder and Ctrl clicking on it. Select Get Info from the subsequent menu and apply the required settings under the Ownership & Permissions heading.

5 Select the required volume and click OK

6 Browse to the Drop Box and view or copy the files that have been placed there

# Sharing an Internet connection

Once you have created a network of two or more computers it can be a considerable benefit to be able to share an Internet connection between them. This means that two, or more, people can use a single Internet connection at the same time.

*Cable/DSL routers can be used to access the Internet through a dial-up connection, not just for cable or DSL access.*

## Hardware method of sharing

One way to share an Internet connection is to use a device known as a cable/DSL router. This is connected to your Internet connection at one end and all of your networked computers at the other through Ethernet cables (providing there are enough Ethernet ports for all of your machines). The router serves the role of connecting the Internet and all of the networked machines.

*If you have two computers networked via an Ethernet cable, the router serves as the connection between them: each machine has a cable that attaches to the router.*

## Software method of sharing

Using OS X it is also possible to share an Internet connection from one computer to others on your network. To do this, connect your computer to your Internet connection at one end, via an Ethernet cable or to a dial-up modem. Then, connect the computer with the Internet connection to another machine (or a hub or switch if you want to share it with more than one machine.) The relevant software settings can then be applied in the Sharing preference within System Preferences:

*If you are sharing a cable or DSL Internet connection with the software method, the computer connecting to the Internet requires two Ethernet ports, one for the Internet connection and one to connect to the rest of the network.*

1 Click on the Internet tab

3 Click Start to begin Internet sharing

2 Select the Ethernet options

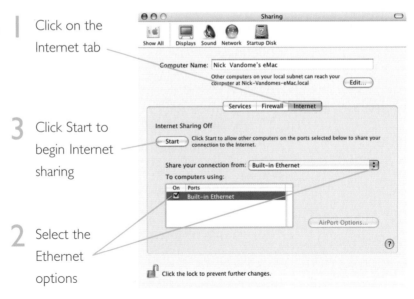

# Maintaining OS X

Even though OS X lives up to the claim of being extremely stable, it still benefits from a robust maintenance regime. This chapter looks at some of the tasks that can be performed to keep OS X in top shape and it also covers some general troubleshooting issues that could occur.

## Covers

Chapter Ten

# Disk Utility

Disk Utility is a utility program that allows you to perform certain testing and repair functions for OS X. It incorporates a variety of functions and it is a good option for general maintenance and if your computer is not running as it should.

Each of the functions within Disk Utility can be applied to specific drives and volumes. However, it is not possible to use the OS X start-up disk within Disk Utility, as this will be in operation to run the program, and Disk Utility cannot operate on a disk that has programs already running. To use Disk Utility:

*Disk Utility is located within the Applications> Utilities folder.*

## Checking disks

*The start-up disk is automatically checked when OS X is booted up.*

Click the First Aid tab to check a disk

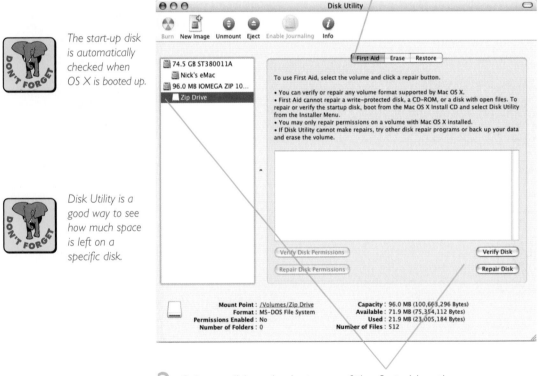

*Disk Utility is a good way to see how much space is left on a specific disk.*

2 Select a disk and select one of the first aid options

## Erasing a disk

To erase all of the data on a disk or a volume:

1 Click on the
Erase tab
and select a
disk or a
volume

*If there is a problem with a disk and OS X can fix it, the Repair button will be available. Click on this to enable Disk Utility to repair the problem.*

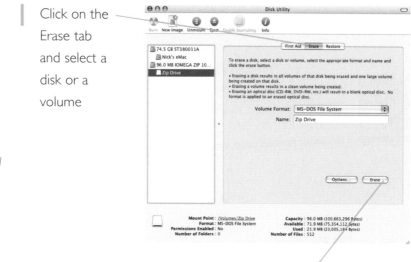

2 Click Erase to erase the data on the selected disk or volume

## Partitioning a disk

To create additional partitions on a disk or a volume:

*If you erase data from a removable disk, such as a Zip disk or a CD, you will not be able to retrieve it.*

1 Click on the
Partition tab
and select a
disk or volume

*Partitions are separate areas within a disk or volume. This does not change the overall size of the item but it can help to organize your data.*

2 Select
options for
partitioning

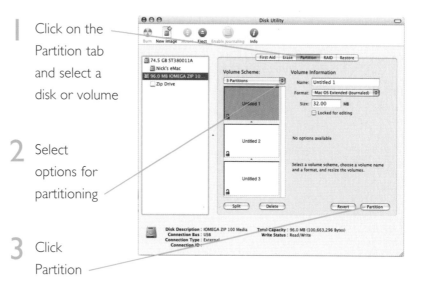

3 Click
Partition

# System Profiler

System Profiler is a utility program that can be used to view information about the hardware and software installed on your computer. It can give valuable information about how your system is running and if there are any problems with any elements of your computer. To use System Profiler:

*System Profiler is located within the Applications> Utilities folder.*

**1** Click here to obtain details of internal and external hardware devices

**2** Details of hardware devices are displayed here

**3** Click here to obtain details of software programs on your computer

**4** Details of software programs are displayed here

# Activity Monitor

Activity Monitor is a utility program that can be used to view information about how much processing power and memory are being used to run programs. This can be useful to know if certain programs are running slowly or crashing frequently. To use Activity Monitor:

*Activity Monitor is located within the Applications> Utilities folder.*

1 Click here to see how much processing power a certain application is using

*Select the Network tab to see how your network connection is operating i.e. how much data it has downloaded and the speed of the connection.*

2 Click here to see how much system memory is being used while a certain application is in use

# Updating software

Nothing in the world of computing stands still for long and this is particularly true of software, which is being updated continually. To make sure that you always have the latest versions of the Apple programs on your system it is possible to have updates sent to your computer as they are released. To do this:

1 In System Preferences, double-click on the Software Update icon

**Software Update**

*In a lot of cases, software updates will be downloaded and installed automatically.*

2 Set the preferences for obtaining software updates automatically. Click Check Now for recent updates

*For some software updates, such as those to OS X itself, you may have to restart your computer for them to take effect.*

3 Once an update has been downloaded, double-click on this icon to access the installation folder

Backup_2.0.1.dmg

4 Double-click here to install the program or update

# Restoring preferences

One factor that can cause problems with a program is if its Preferences folder becomes corrupted. This was a particular problem with OS 9 and earlier, but it can still occur with OS X. If a program is crashing a lot then you can try removing its Preferences folder and closing down the program. The next time it is opened, OS X will create a new Preferences folder that should be corruption free. To do this:

1 Click on the Finder icon on the Dock and click on your Home folder

The problem of corrupted Preferences folders is a lot less common in OS X than in earlier versions of Mac operating systems.

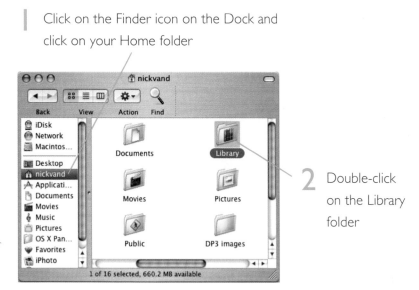

2 Double-click on the Library folder

3 Double-click on the Preferences folder

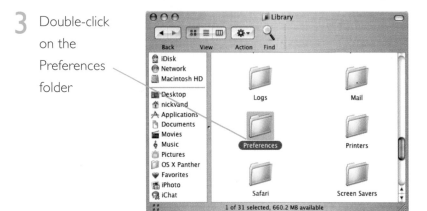

4 Select the Preferences folder of the program that is causing problems

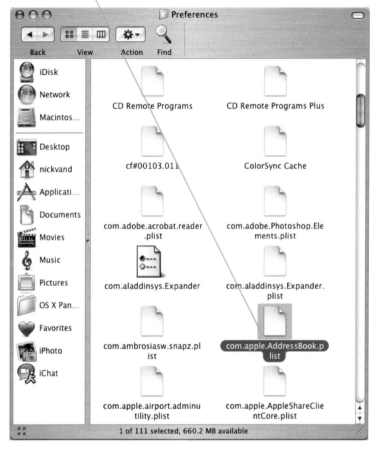

*If you have several programs running when a problem occurs, delete all of the relevant Preferences folders in turn. After deleting each one, open the programs to see if the problem has been resolved. If not, repeat the process with another Preferences folder. In this way you should be able to isolate the program with the problem. After each Preferences folder has been removed to the Trash, you will have to reboot your computer so that OS X can create a new Preferences folder for that program.*

5 Drag the Preferences folder into the Trash. Close the program and then reboot it

# Problems with programs

### The simple answer

OS X is something of a rarity in the world of computing software: it claims to be remarkably stable, and it is. However, this is not to say that things do not sometimes go wrong, although this is considerably less frequent than with older Mac operating systems. Sometimes this will be due to problems within particular programs and on occasions the problems may lie with OS X itself. If this does happen the first course of action is to close down OS X using the Apple menu>Shut Down command. Then restart the computer. If this does not work, or you cannot access the Shut Down command, try turning off the power to the computer and then starting up again.

### Force quitting

If a particular program is not responding it can be closed down separately without the need to reboot the computer. To do this:

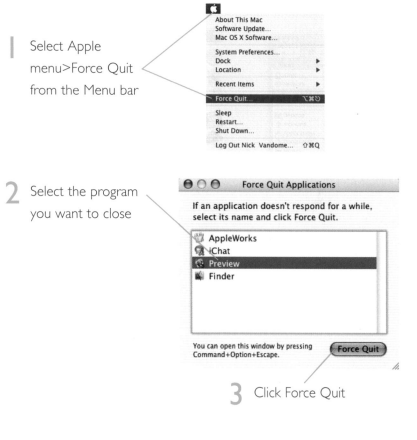

Select Apple menu>Force Quit from the Menu bar

2 Select the program you want to close

3 Click Force Quit

# General troubleshooting

It is true that things do go wrong with OS X, although probably with less regularity than with some other operating systems. If something does go wrong, there are a number of items that you can check and also take some steps to ensure that you do not lose any important data if the worst case scenario occurs and your hard drive packs up completely.

- Back up. If everything does go wrong it is essential to take preventative action in the form of making sure that all of your data is backed up and saved. This can either be done with the Backup program available from the .Mac service or by backing up manually by copying data to a CD or DVD

*In extreme cases, you will not be able to reboot your computer normally. If this happens, you will have to pull out the power cable and reattach it. You will then be able to reboot, although the computer may want to check its hard drive to make sure that everything is in working order.*

- Reboot. One traditional reply by IT helpdesks is to reboot i.e. turn off the computer and turn it back on again and hope that the problem has resolved itself. In a lot of cases this simple operation does the trick but it is not always a viable solution for major problems

- Check cables. If the problem appears to be with a network connection or an externally connected device, check that all cables are connected properly and have not worked loose. If possible, make sure that all cables are tucked away so that they cannot inadvertently be pulled out

- Check network settings. If your network or Internet connections are not working, check the network setting in System Preferences. Sometimes when you make a change to one item this can have an adverse effect on one of these settings. (If possible, lock the settings once you have applied them, by clicking on the padlock icon in the Network preferences window)

- Check for viruses. If your computer is infected with a virus this could effect the efficient running of the machine. Luckily this is less of a problem for Macs as virus writers tend to concentrate their efforts towards Windows-based machines. However, there are plenty of Mac viruses out there, so make sure your computer is protected by the .Mac virus program, Virex, or a program such as Norton AntiVirus which is available from www.symantec.com

- Check Start-up items. If you have set certain items to start automatically when your computer is turned on, this could cause certain conflicts within your machine. If this is the case, disable the items from launching during the booting up of the computer. This can be done within the Accounts preference of System Preferences by clicking on the Startup Items tab, selecting the relevant item and pressing the minus button

- Check permissions. If you, or other users, are having problems opening items this could be because of the permissions that are set. To check these, select the item in the Finder, click on the Actions button on the Finder toolbar and select Get Info. In the Ownership & Permissions section of the Info window you will be able to set the relevant permissions to allow other users, or yourself, to read, write or have no access

Click here to view permissions settings

- Eject external devices. Sometimes external devices, such as Zip drives, can become temperamental and refuse to eject the disks within them, or even show up on the desktop or in the Finder. If this happens you can eject the disk by pressing the mouse button when the Mac chimes are heard during the booting up process

- Turn-off your screen saver. Screen savers can sometimes cause conflicts within your computer, particularly if they have been downloaded from an unreliable source. If this happens, change the screen saver within the Desktop & Screen Saver preference of the System Preferences or disable it altogether

# Restoring software

There may be some instances when you want to restore some of the software that came with OS X, such as if you have deleted a program and then you realize that you require it after all. This can be done with one of the CDs that comes with OS X. However, this does not reinstall OS X itself. To do this you should use the OS X Installation CD and hold down the C key when the Mac chimes are heard. Then follow the installation procedure in the same way as installing the software for the first time. To restore software that came with OS X:

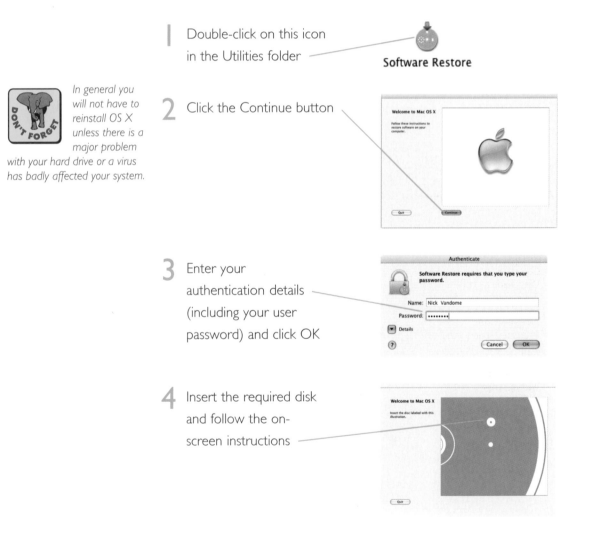

1 Double-click on this icon in the Utilities folder

**Software Restore**

*In general you will not have to reinstall OS X unless there is a major problem with your hard drive or a virus has badly affected your system.*

2 Click the Continue button

Welcome to Mac OS X

Follow these instructions to restore software on your computer.

Quit    Continue

3 Enter your authentication details (including your user password) and click OK

Authenticate

Software Restore requires that you type your password.

Name: Nick Vandome
Password: •••••••

Details

Cancel    OK

4 Insert the required disk and follow the on-screen instructions

Welcome to Mac OS X

Insert the disc labeled with this illustration.

Quit

# Index

# O

# P

# Q

# R

# S